Alleluia
to **Amen**

"Empowering our student leaders in college ministry settings requires equipping them with materials that will help them become stronger leaders. Justin McClain's *Alleluia to Amen* is a resource that aids our student parishioners in becoming more confident in both individual and group prayers. The book's easy format and breadth of prayers allows for people in different stages of their faith journey to be confident in leading prayers for any occasion."

Rosie Chinea Shawver
Director of Campus Ministry
Our Savior Parish and USC Caruso Catholic Center

"Pray without ceasing. St. Paul said it. The Church recommends it. And Justin McClain's new book helps us accomplish it. Never again be at a loss for words of prayer in a parish setting. *Alleluia to Amen* assists those in leadership and supportive roles to find the right words to call God's people to prayer. It is immensely practical and filled with the Spirit. It makes a great gift for parish clergy, catechists, teachers, group leaders, and even Catholic families."

Pat Gohn
Editor of *Catechist*

"Alleluia, indeed! This wonderful collection of prayers is what every parish needs in its library: a fresh, contemporary, and winningly accessible compendium of hope, praise, petition, and thanksgiving. I'm giving this to every priest, deacon, and catechist I know. This book will be used again and again, and can turn almost every occasion into an opportunity to pray. We need that in our world—now, more than ever. Amen!"

Deacon Greg Kandra
Journalist and blogger at *The Deacon's Bench*

"In *Alleluia to Amen: The Prayer Book for Catholic Parishes*, Justin McClain has taken up the challenge of reuniting liturgy and everyday life. This is a book that can help parishes around the county learn to once again sanctify each moment of time. It is precisely the kind of book that allows even us busy twenty-first-century Catholics to pray—as best as we are able—constantly."

From the foreword by **Timothy P. O'Malley**
Director of Education
McGrath Institute for Church Life
University of Notre Dame

Alleluia *to* **Amen**

THE PRAYER BOOK FOR
CATHOLIC PARISHES

Written and Compiled by **Justin McClain**

AVE MARIA PRESS AVE Notre Dame, Indiana

Founded in 1865, Ave Maria Press is a ministry of the United States Province of Holy Cross.

www.avemariapress.com

Paperback: ISBN-13 978-1-59471-927-1

E-book: ISBN-13 978-1-59471-928-8

Cover image © Andreas von Einsiedel / Alamy Stock Photox.

Cover and text design by Samantha Watson.

Printed and bound in the United States of America.

Library of Congress Cataloging-in-Publication Data is available.

Contents

Foreword

In the context of how to order the life of the local Church, Paul writes, "Rejoice always, pray constantly, give thanks in all circumstances; for this is the will of God in Christ Jesus for you" (1 Thes 5:16–18).

The early Church took seriously Paul's exhortation to pray constantly. Monks left behind the cities to pray through the Psalter each day. Within the cities themselves, the bishop would gather with the faithful to sing Morning and Evening Prayer. Lay Christians would wake up in the middle of the night to offer prayers and spiritual hymns to Christ. The act of worship permeated every dimension of Christian life, whether one was a cleric, a consecrated religious, or a layperson.

In medieval Catholicism, the order of prayer for monks became more complicated. Lay Catholics—at least those wealthy enough to own books—wanted access to the prayer of the monks. The Books of Hours adapted the Liturgy of the Hours for use by laypeople. There were selections of psalms, devotional prayers, and illuminations that placed the central figures of salvation history in the context of the time period and city where the prayer book was produced.

The liturgical calendars of these prayer books were often decorated with scenes from daily life. An early sixteenth-century prayer book from Belgium is an extraordinary example of this union of prayer and daily life. The section for February shows an image of a man chopping wood. In April, a woman picks flowers in a garden. In November, a pig is slaughtered, while in December, a snowball fight breaks out.

The union of day-to-day imagery and the sanctoral cycle of the Church is no accident! The tasks of life in the world take place alongside the feasts of the Church year. As the medieval Church celebrated the Presentation of the Lord in February, wood had to be chopped to keep people warm. Christians knew that everyday human activities such as plowing the fields, snowball fights, and even courtship all unfolded in a world in which the Word became flesh and dwelt among us. All time, all human activity, has been transformed through the Incarnation of Jesus Christ.

In the early modern age, this union of daily life and the liturgy began to weaken. The feasts of the Church year competed with a new sort of economic life. Factories were not shut down for the feasts of the Church, since this would mean a loss of money. "Going to church" was an essential activity for a respectable citizen on Sunday, but the rest of the week (especially for men) was ordered to politics and work.

In the nineteenth and twentieth centuries, the liturgical movement sought to reconnect daily life to the liturgy. The goal was not simply to reform the rites of the Church, making them comprehensible for the contemporary person, but rather to bring together liturgical prayer and daily life once again.

There were efforts to transform the domestic space into a place infused with liturgical practice. Feast days were to be celebrated with special meals, prayers, and chants. Groups of lawyers, health care professionals, and students formed study groups where they discussed ways of infusing daily life with the spirit of the liturgy. The University of Notre Dame for the first time offered courses in theological education on how to participate fruitfully in the prayer of the liturgy.

Sadly, in the twenty-first century, the gap between liturgy and life has grown larger still. The feasts of the Church year are not known by many Catholics in the pews. The fissure between Sunday eucharistic practice and the rest of life has only increased. As we grow busier, as everything speeds up, how are we to rediscover a way of sanctifying everyday life? The weekend should never be just an opportunity to participate in leisure activities related to consumerism and entertainment. Rather, it is to be a time to give thanks to God for rest and for communion with one another in our homes and in our parishes. Daily life is offered back to God through prayers that are accessible, attuned to the liturgical seasons, and related to every dimension of our Catholic lives.

In *Alleluia to Amen: The Prayer Book for Catholic Parishes*, Justin McClain has taken up the challenge of reuniting liturgy and everyday life. This is a book that can help parishes around the country learn to once again sanctify each moment of time. It is precisely the kind of book that allows even us busy twenty-first-century Catholics to pray—as best as we are able—constantly.

Timothy P. O'Malley, PhD
Director of Education, McGrath Institute for Church Life
University of Notre Dame

Introduction

The heart of the Church resides in our parishes—the foundational centers from which we Catholics draw our identity, nourishment, and mission as disciples of Jesus Christ. Parishes are where we meet God in Word and sacrament, in the ordained ministers of the Church, and in the lay faithful. We gather in parishes to pray daily, weekly, and for particular occasions, both planned and unexpected. Parish prayer marks our coming and our going, our work and our play, our need for comfort and our great rejoicing. Prayer teaches us who we are and points us toward becoming more. In the seemingly constant motion of busy lives, we seek and find refuge in our parish churches and in our communities wherein the Lord himself resides.

Every parish hosts various people, activities, ministries, and events. We regularly gather to pray the Church's liturgy, of course, but we also gather for and pray at meetings, social events, service projects, dedications of new buildings, times of crisis and sorrow, and days of great rejoicing. As disciples of Christ, members of his Body, we must be rooted in and remain guided by prayer in all we do together as the Church. When the parish community is animated, challenged, and nourished by an enduring commitment to communal prayer, we are empowered to live and spread the Gospel, to evangelize. That is where this book comes in.

Called to Lead and Pray

The prayers of *Alleluia to Amen* supplement and are never meant to replace the Church's liturgical celebrations, which anchor the spiritual life of the parish. They seek to draw the parish community closer to Christ and to one another in the interest of fellowship based on fidelity, reflective of the words of St. Paul to the Christian community at Corinth: "God is faithful, by whom you were called into the fellowship with his Son, Jesus Christ our Lord" (1 Cor 1:9).

These prayers can be used for a variety of needs and in many circumstances in the life of a parish. Of course, impromptu prayers are reliably useful as well, but at times you may find that you don't have the clarity of mind or even the energy to pray spontaneously in a manner suitable to the occasion. Catholics are accustomed to worshipping together—our public prayer—and so many times you will realize that an already-composed prayer is just what you want. The prayers in this book are for those times.

Laypeople and clergy alike will find here a treasury of options for parish prayers. Anyone called to lead a group within the parish ought to feel comfortable using and, when needed, adapting these prayers to strengthen the life of the parish. The topical index at the back of the book will help you locate just the right ones, and the appendix will help you learn to develop your own prayers for times when that approach will be more helpful.

May our parish communities "rejoice always, [and] pray constantly" (1 Thes 5:16–17)!

1.

Days of the Week

SUNDAY MORNING

Lord Jesus Christ, we praise and thank you for the gift of joy as we begin this new day and welcome the beginning of a new week filled with promise. Fill us with hope, and be with us in our joys and in our challenges. Strengthen us to serve you and to bring the good news of your salvation to everyone we meet. We ask this in your holy name. Amen.

SUNDAY AFTERNOON

Lord God, be with us on this Sunday afternoon, halfway through the holiest day of the week. May the remainder of our day feature rest and peace, and may we seek to do your will both in the rest of today and in the week ahead. Bless the parishioners of this community as we give thanks for the eucharistic sacrifice offered by your Son, in whose name we pray. Amen.

SUNDAY EVENING

Dear Lord, as this day dedicated to celebrating your Resurrection draws to a close, we give you thanks for all that you have given us. Please strengthen us to face the week ahead, and make us eager to meditate on your goodness as we proclaim it to a world longing for your abiding love. May we always strive to do your will as we endeavor to make you known, loved, and served. We ask this through Christ the Lord. Amen.

SUNDAY NIGHT

Heavenly Father, grant us restful slumber and peace of heart and mind as we prepare for the week ahead. Help us to remain focused on you during this week. Help us to remain joyful and zealous when it comes to seeking opportunities to follow your holy will. We ask this in the name of Jesus Christ, your Son. Amen.

MONDAY

MONDAY MORNING

Lord God, as the workweek begins, we dedicate this time to you. Help us to order our priorities around your will so that we can form our decisions around what is fitting for the kingdom of God. Help us to be of one accord with our peers so that we can work together and collaborate in the best interest of our mission. Lead us to strive for peace and goodwill throughout this week. In Jesus' name, we pray. Amen.

Monday Afternoon

Heavenly Father, guide us to do your will in the midst of all that we face. May we seek multiple opportunities to bring the Good News of your Son Jesus Christ into the world, endeavoring to draw others to regard him as the main priority in life. Thank you for the many blessings that you have given us so far this week, whether or not we have realized it. In Christ's name, we pray. Amen.

Monday Evening

Lord Jesus Christ, as the first day of the workweek draws to a close, please give us the strength and fervor to persevere in our responsibilities. Help us to prioritize the sacramental life, centered on the Mass, throughout this week. Please draw us to appreciate and celebrate family life, spending time with our loved ones. We ask this in your holy name. Amen.

Monday Night

Dear Lord, on this first night of the workweek, lead us to find rest in you, recalling that you are the only source of the true joy that we are all seeking. Inspire us to reflect on today's successes so that we can continue to look for creative ways to bring you glory and honor. Grant us a good night's sleep so that tomorrow will be yet another opportunity to serve you and do your will. We ask this in Christ's name. Amen.

TUESDAY

Tuesday Morning

Heavenly Father, please be with us as we make our way through this week. In the highs and the lows that we encounter, let us praise you for the many gifts you have given us. Throughout today, help us to labor collaboratively with our fellow workers in the vineyard. Draw us ever closer to doing your will this day so that we can give you greater glory in all that we do. We ask this in Christ's name. Amen.

Tuesday Afternoon

Heavenly Father, as we approach the midpoint of this week, help us remain productive in our duties. More importantly, please allow us to reflect on how we can use our remaining time this week to take advantage of the numerous opportunities to serve, glorify, honor, and adore you. We ask this in the holy name of Jesus Christ the Lord. Amen.

Tuesday Evening

Heavenly Father, as this day winds down, please be with us. Watch over us in the midst of the many other tasks that remain for us to complete this week. Let us be sure to look at your will intently as we go about them. We ask this in the holy name of Jesus Christ the Lord. Amen.

TUESDAY NIGHT

Lord Jesus Christ, as this day closes, let us reflect on the many moments from today for which we can be grateful, even in the midst of seeming trials. Be with us as we conclude the first part of the week and look forward to what awaits us in the middle part. Grant us restful sleep so that we can serve you with a renewed and refreshed perspective. We ask this in your holy name. Amen.

WEDNESDAY

WEDNESDAY MORNING

Lord, we give thanks that we are halfway through the week. May our hearts be glad with all the good we have done this week and remain eager to serve you and your kingdom ever more fully through the rest of this week. We thank you for all that you have given us and ask that you shower us with the gift of heartfelt gratitude. We pray this in Christ's name. Amen.

WEDNESDAY AFTERNOON

Lord God, at the midpoint of the week, we give you thanks for the many chances that we will have this week to magnify your kingdom. Send forth the Holy Spirit to inspire us, especially if we are facing weariness, illness, busy schedules, or other trials.

We ask you to make us ever open to the good works that you would like to do in our lives. Amen.

WEDNESDAY EVENING

Lord God, here in the middle portion of the week, we thank you for the many blessings that you have bestowed upon us. We likewise ask you to be with us, to strengthen us to face the many other tasks that remain to be completed. Help us look forward in joyful trust to what the rest of the week will bring, and help us to look at every day as a unique opportunity to be of service to you. We ask this in Christ's holy name. Amen.

WEDNESDAY NIGHT

Lord God, here in the middle of the week, we give you thanks for bringing us to the conclusion of another day. As we look ahead, please give us strength to accomplish all that we have to do, ensuring that we are working for your kingdom and not for fleeting temporal concerns. Grant us peaceful rest. We pray this in Jesus' holy name. Amen.

THURSDAY

THURSDAY MORNING

Almighty Father, be with us today. Help us to reflect on and learn from what has occurred earlier this week, and guide us to look for ever more creative and efficient ways of serving you, in the ultimate interest of the kingdom of God. We ask this in the precious name of your Son, the Lord Jesus Christ. Amen.

THURSDAY AFTERNOON

Lord God, as the week begins to wind down, help us focus on what we have set out to accomplish. Although we may feel inundated with responsibilities, we must remain focused on you as the source of our joy, comfort, and peace. May we look forward to the restful time with loved ones that will hopefully come this weekend. We ask this in Jesus' name. Amen.

THURSDAY EVENING

Lord Jesus Christ, it was on a Thursday evening that you sat down at the Last Supper with your disciples, instituting the Sacraments of Holy Orders and the Eucharist. Let us always remain grateful for the priests in our lives—holy men at your sacramental service. And let us never take for granted the divine gift that is the Eucharist: your Body, Blood, Soul, and Divinity. We make this prayer in your sacred name. Amen.

THURSDAY NIGHT

Lord Jesus Christ, it was on a Thursday night that you entered into the misery of your Passion, after you were betrayed for mere money and arrested. As this day concludes, be with us as we strive to make sure that our goal is never human success, which fades away, but rather the glory of your kingdom. Please grant us rest as we open our hearts and minds to your sacrificial love for us. We pray in deepest gratitude. Amen.

FRIDAY

FRIDAY MORNING

Dear Lord, as the workweek draws to a close, teach us to embrace your presence among us. Give us cheerful hearts and sufficient energy, not for the sake of productivity alone, but so that we can devote this day to serving you in many different ways. Teach us to learn from the many blessings you have granted us this week. In Jesus' name, we pray. Amen.

FRIDAY AFTERNOON

Lord Jesus Christ, we pause to recall your Passion and Death every Friday afternoon. Please help us to honor your sacrifice by looking for opportunities to serve one another and all whom we encounter. In gratitude for your profound act of self-emptying sacrifice, may we strive to glorify you throughout the rest of this day and the weekend ahead. We ask this in your holy name. Amen.

FRIDAY EVENING

Precious Lord Jesus Christ, we it was on a Friday evening that your body was placed in a cold, dark tomb after it was taken down from the Cross. At the time, your followers did not know the Resurrection was to follow. Receive into paradise the souls of all the faithful who have died. May they participate fully in the glory of heaven as we, with them, wait in joyful hope for the coming of your kingdom. In gratitude and hope, we pray. Amen.

FRIDAY NIGHT

Lord Jesus Christ, your followers were probably terrified on the night of Good Friday, as they had just seen your brutal mistreatment and death at the hands of sinful men and knew that they were also now targets. May we never lose faith in you, and give us the fortitude and courage necessary to bring you into the world, during the coming weekend and beyond. We make this prayer in your holy name. Amen.

FOR A RESTFUL WEEKEND

Dear Lord, sometimes the week can be very challenging and busy. Provide us with a weekend that is both restful and refreshing so that we may recuperate and use our renewed energy to better serve you. May this weekend, especially Mass on Sunday, serve as an opportunity to reorient our focus back to you and your divine will. We ask this in the name of Jesus the Lord. Amen.

FOR THOSE TRAVELING THIS WEEKEND

Heavenly Father, watch over those who are traveling out of the area this weekend. Grant them safety, peace, and comfort as they make their way to their destination. No matter the cause of their travel, may they know of the prayers of this parish community, and upon their return, may they be welcomed with open arms. We ask this in Jesus' name. Amen.

SATURDAY

SATURDAY MORNING

Dear Lord, we thank you for bringing us to this new day. During this weekend, please help us to look for opportunities to serve you and to gain rest in order to make us more effective in our various ministries. To all who will serve our parish community this weekend, give joyful spirits and clear minds. May we welcome all who gather here to worship you and for fellowship. May each of us use our time this weekend for your greater glory. Amen.

SATURDAY AFTERNOON

Lord God, a Saturday afternoon can be one of the most restful and relaxing times of the week for many of your people. We pray for their renewal in your love. Look upon all of us with loving care as we embrace your wondrous love and graciously accept your many blessings. We ask this in Christ's name. Amen.

SATURDAY EVENING

Heavenly Father, as the week draws to a close, we ask you to be with us. Especially for those of us who are spending time with family, friends, and other loved ones, allow this to be a time of fellowship in the interest of the ministerial opportunities that abound. Please give us graceful rest. We ask this in Jesus' holy name. Amen.

SATURDAY NIGHT

Heavenly Father, we give you thanks for your multiple gifts. Let us never attempt to worship you with anything other than a full, grateful heart. May we value the remainder of this weekend, ideally as an opportunity to be with family and friends. Let us look forward to the Easter joy that each Sunday promises, and move with hope into the coming week. We ask this in Jesus' name. Amen.

2.

Seasons and Movable Feasts

The Natural Seasons

WINTER

In Gratitude for the Quiet of Winter

We give thanks to you, Father in heaven, for the gift of quiet and solitude during the winter season. As earth rests and awaits the newness of spring may we find renewed peace of mind and heart. May we listen to you and open ourselves to your holy will in our lives. No matter where we find ourselves during this winter season, may this unique time of year draw us closer to you and the work of your kingdom. We pray this in Jesus' name. Amen.

For Those Battling Illness during the Winter

Healing Lord, be with those who are battling some sort of illness this winter, whether a relatively minor sickness or a more prolonged and chronic condition. May they know healing of mind, body, and ultimately spirit, especially if they are facing hopelessness and despair. May they recover their strength to be able to serve you more fully. We ask this in Christ's name. Amen.

For Those Driving in Ice and Snow

Dear Lord, guard and protect those who are traveling in icy or snowy conditions. Place your guiding hand over them as they travel so that they may arrive safely. Inspire them to exercise prudence and to recognize the limitations of their driving abilities. We ask this in Jesus' holy name. Amen.

For Road Crews

Heavenly Father, watch over, protect, and guide the road crews who are operating in often challenging conditions during the winter months. Lead them to safe paths and provide them with the courage to make the roadways that they traverse safer for other travelers. Let us give thanks for the role that they play in safeguarding our passage. We ask this in Jesus' holy name. Amen.

For Those Who Are Living in the Cold

Merciful Father, we pray that you may watch over all those who are living in cold conditions, especially those who are homeless or without adequate heat. May they find warmth. May those who are able to provide shelter do so, knowing they are offering shelter to Christ himself. We ask this in the name of Jesus Christ the Lord. Amen.

For Safety during a Winter Storm

Lord God, we implore you to keep us safe during the winter storm now threatening our area. Please watch over and protect our families, friends, and neighbors so that we can continue to glorify your holy will. We ask this in the name of Jesus the Lord, who shepherds our souls to security by inviting us to accept his wonderful gift of salvation. Amen.

SPRING

In Gratitude for the Hope of Spring

Lord God of hopefulness, the spring is a rewarding time of year during which we give thanks for life, newness, and reconciliation. Guide us to remain grateful for the promises that you have given us, and draw us to use this season to more effectively magnify your holy and righteous kingdom. We ask this through the Lord of Life. Amen.

In Gratitude for Clearer Weather

Dear Lord, we thank you for the clearer weather that we are experiencing with the springtime. May we look at the new life that comes forth in nature as an opportunity to glory in your creation and to recall that you are the source and goal of our lives. Renew our hearts, and open our eyes to the many chances that we have to open our hearts to your refreshing love. We pray this in Jesus' name. Amen.

For Landscapers Working on the Parish Property

Lord God, watch over the landscaping staff who are working to beautify the grounds of this parish community. May we remain ever grateful for the labors that they undertake throughout the year, especially during the spring, summer, and fall, to make the parish property visually appealing so that we can focus even better on the beautiful transformation that you undertake in our hearts. In Jesus' name, we pray. Amen.

For Parishioners Who Are Planting and Gardening

Lord of Life, guide the hands of those parishioners who are planting and gardening, whether at the parish, at their residences, or in other areas. May their flowers, crops, and other plantings be fruitful, and even more importantly, may the bounty be a reminder for them to give you thanks and magnify your kingdom. We ask this in Jesus' holy name. Amen.

Celebrating the End of School

Lord God, as the school year ends and we look forward to the restfulness of the summer, help all students to remember the lessons that they have learned, the most important of which are those that alert them to your presence in their lives and to your holy call. Please grant the same to all teachers, parents, alumni, volunteers, coaches, and other members of [our parish school] and our [other] local school communities. We ask this in the holy name of Jesus Christ the Lord. Amen.

IN THANKSGIVING FOR TEACHERS AND ALL SCHOOL PERSONNEL

Thank you, Lord in heaven above, for the gift of the educators who serve our community. Classroom teachers, administrators, staff members, volunteers, custodial staff, or other institutional personnel—we give you thanks for their rewarding presence in our school community. Draw them to further your holy will. Amen.

SUMMER

IN GRATITUDE FOR SUMMER WARMTH AND LONG DAYLIGHT

Graceful Father, we express our gratitude to you for the warmth of the summer months and for the longer daylight that permits us to do more throughout the day in service to your holy will. Teach us to moderate our activity so that we do not overexert ourselves. May we use this time to bring you greater glory, in the interest of your kingdom. In Jesus' name, we pray. Amen.

For a Plentiful Growing Season

Provident Father, we ask you to bless this growing season so that our produce is bountiful—not for our own sake, but rather so that we can be more generous stewards of the multiple gifts that you have given us. Inspire us to open our hands to those in the greatest need so that our charity can ultimately contribute to your holy kingdom. We ask this in Jesus' name. Amen.

For a Restful Summer

Lord God, we come to you today to ask for your blessings upon us this summer. Grant us a restful summer so that we may use these months to reconnect with family and friends. Help us to find rejuvenation in you so that we can use our time and energy to better serve you and thus glorify your kingdom. We ask this in the name of Christ the Lord. Amen.

For Those Leaving on Summer Vacation

Heavenly Father, please accompany those who are departing on summer vacation as they travel to their destination, while they are there, and as they return. Grant them renewal of mind, body, and spirit so that they can ably serve you. May they be welcomed by local parishes to celebrate the Eucharist with joy while they are away. We ask this in the name of your Son Jesus Christ. Amen.

For Those Who Suffer in Extreme Heat

Merciful Lord, be with those who are enduring the summer heat at this time, especially the homeless, the elderly, and those without adequate cooling. Give them patience and keep them safe. May the Holy Spirit inspire the rest of us to serve them in whatever needs they have. We ask this in Christ's holy name. Amen.

For Safety during Summer Storms

Lord most high, the power of your creation ever reminds us of your glory. When thunderstorms, tornadoes, and hurricanes threaten, may we turn to you for comfort and clear minds. Give us courage and help us to find shelter for ourselves, our loved ones, and our neighbors. Keep us safe, O Lord, and shower your mercy upon us. Amen.

In Thanksgiving for Garden Produce

Father, we come to you with grateful hearts for the prospect of bounty that we pray you may provide to us through our planting. If this is in accord with your holy will, please grant us a bountiful collection of produce so that we can in turn practice the virtue of charity by sharing it with our neighbors. We ask this in Jesus' divine name. Amen.

FALL

For Returning to School

Loving God, as students return to school, please bless in a special way all who are involved in the ministry of Catholic education. Grant prudence, wisdom, and clarity of mind and heart to the staff who participate in this blessed endeavor. May the Sacred Heart of Jesus reign in the life of every member of the school community, in order to foster reverence and fidelity. In Jesus' name, we pray. Amen.

In Gratitude for Routines

Lord God, we can often find ourselves getting stuck in ruts. On the other hand, we can sometimes find ourselves growing restless and lacking focus. As lighter summer schedules draw to an end, help us to enter into routines that free us to serve you with greater order and peace of mind. We ask this through Jesus' holy name. Amen.

For Partnership between Parishes and Schools

Lord Jesus Christ, you are the center of the activities of both this parish and every Catholic educational institution. Foster a dynamic partnership between all Catholic parishes and Catholic schools so that we can be more receptive to how you are calling us to serve. Bless all parish and school staff to more effectively evangelize and serve as disciples. We ask this in your divine name. Amen.

For a Successful Harvest

Generous Lord, we come to you at this time to pray that you may grant us a bountiful harvest. We celebrate your glorious providence as we hope for an abundance of blessings. Open our hearts to be grateful for all that you have given us and to reflect your generosity by sharing readily with our neighbor. We pray in the name of Christ Jesus, Our Lord. Amen.

In Gratitude for Fall Holidays

We give you thanks, Father in heaven, for the autumn when the natural order gives rise to celebrations of remember once and giving thanks for the bounty of the Earth. May we enter into the joy of fall festivals, Halloween, el Día de los Muertos, and Thanksgiving with friends and neighbors. May the fellowship we find in these holidays bind us to our local communities and cause us to praise your goodness throughout each day. We ask this through Jesus the Lord. Amen.

The Liturgical Seasons

ADVENT

AT THE BEGINNING OF ADVENT

Lord Jesus Christ, as we prepare for your Nativity at Christmas, guide our hearts to meditate on the beauty and the wonder of your Incarnation. Draw our thoughts heavenward so that we can better appreciate the gift that was your earthly life, in anticipation of the prospect of eternal life with you. Through the intercession of St. Mary and St. Joseph within your Holy Family, we pray. Amen.

FOR ADVENT MORNINGS

We give thanks to you, Lord Jesus Christ, for the hope and joyful anticipation of the Advent season. Draw us to meditate anew on your Good News this and every Advent morning. Teach us to seek and to follow your holy will throughout this day as we prepare our hearts, minds, and homes for the Christmas celebration of your dwelling among us. In your holy name, we pray. Amen.

FOR ADVENT EVENINGS

Thank you, Lord God above, for this wonderful Advent season, a time of turning back to you, of waiting and longing for your coming each day and in fullness at the end of time. May the stillness of the evening hours help prepare our hearts for the coming of the Prince of Peace. We ask this through the same Jesus Christ the Lord. Amen.

ADVENT WREATH PRAYER

We give you thanks, heavenly Father, for this holy season of Advent during which we await the joyous season of Christmas. Please shower down your blessings on this Advent wreath so that this parish and all our members may see it as a reminder to draw our attention steadily heavenward, meditating ever more profoundly on the wonders of Christ's Incarnation. May its growing light and evergreen branches bring us hope and good cheer as we eagerly await Christmas. We ask this through the Word Incarnate, Jesus, the Lord. Amen.

DECEMBER 8: SOLEMNITY OF THE IMMACULATE CONCEPTION OF THE BLESSED VIRGIN MARY

Lord Jesus Christ, we give thanks for the example of your mother, who was your most faithful follower in your earthly life. As we celebrate Mary's own conception through your Sts. Joachim and Anne, may we imitate her example of fidelity to you and her openness to bearing you into a dark and broken world. We pray in gratitude and hope through the intercession of Mary, virgin and mother. Amen.

THE O ANTIPHONS

December 17
O Wisdom of our God Most High,

guiding creation with power and love:
come to teach us the path of knowledge!

December 18
O Leader of the House of Israel,
giver of the Law to Moses on Sinai:
come to rescue us with your mighty power!

December 19
O Root of Jesse's stem,
sign of God's love for all his people:
come to save us without delay!

December 20
O Key of David,
opening the gates of God's eternal Kingdom:
come and free the prisoners of darkness!

December 21
O Radiant Dawn,
splendor of eternal light, sun of justice:
come and shine on those who dwell in darkness and in the
shadow of death.

December 22
O King of all nations and keystone of the Church:
come and save man, whom you formed from the dust!

December 23
O Emmanuel, our King and Giver of Law:
come to save us, Lord our God!

To Open Las Posadas Navideñas

We thank you, heavenly Father, for the opportunity to celebrate the tradition of Las Posadas during this holy season. As we meditate on what Mary and Joseph endured as they sought shelter in anticipation of Christ's birth, teach us to make room in our hearts for Christ—not only as we recall his birth at Bethlehem, but every day throughout each year. May we always seek him and wait in joyous hope for his coming in glory at the end of time. We ask this in Jesus' holy name. Amen.

At the Conclusion of Advent

Lord Jesus Christ, as Christmas arrives, may we be ever thankful for your entry into the world, into our very humanity. Kindle within our hearts a desire to seek unique ways of announcing the Good News of salvation in you. May we come to flourish in the joy of each Christmas through the divine and salvific light of your reign as Prince of Peace and Light of the World. We ask this through the intercession of St. Mary and St. Joseph. Amen.

CHRISTMAS

In Gratitude for the Incarnation

Lord Jesus, thank you for coming to us, God in human form, drawing humanity's gaze heavenward and into your loving embrace on that first holy night in Bethlehem. May we always contemplate your Incarnation with renewed desire to know, love, and serve you here on earth so that we may share eternal glory with you one day in heaven. Reside within our hearts and our homes during this joyous Christmas season, when we honor you, the Christ Child, and look forward to your coming each day and in fullness at the end of the ages. Amen.

FOR THOSE IN NEED AT CHRISTMASTIME

Heavenly Father, help us to open our hearts and our hands to those in our community who are struggling this Christmas season. When our loved ones and neighbors struggle with material need; with physical or mental illnesses; or with grief, loneliness, anxiety, or distress, teach us to care for them and accompany them as we are able. May we be both considerate and generous so that those living in need will experience the warmth of your love, delivered by us as your disciples. We ask this through Christ the Lord. Amen.

DECEMBER 26: FEAST OF ST. STEPHEN, THE FIRST MARTYR

Lord Jesus Christ, your servant St. Stephen became singularly devoted to you while a young man, as the Church was expanding in the time after your earthly ministry. His example of courage, even in the face of martyrdom, drew many to love you and your Church. May we act with similar grace and fortitude in the face of our own adversities, always remaining devoted to following your holy will. Through the intercession of St. Stephen, we pray. Amen.

DECEMBER 27: FEAST OF ST. JOHN, APOSTLE AND EVANGELIST

Jesus Christ, Word Made Flesh, our Lord and our God, lead us to imitate the saintly example of your apostle and evangelist, St. John. May we meditate on the beauty of following your precepts and faithfully spread your Good News abroad, drawing others to your divine presence. We ask this in your righteous name. Amen.

DECEMBER 28: FEAST OF THE HOLY INNOCENTS, MARTYRS

Lord God who created the universe, you chose to step into our humanity in the form of a tiny infant. Inspire, both inside and outside of the Church, a greater respect for all human life, beginning at conception and through natural death. Grant us, your Church, clarity of purpose, courage, and creative energy to confront the neglect and abuse of the most innocent of our world, born and unborn. Teach us to work for justice and the protection of all human life. Amen.

DECEMBER 29: MEMORIAL OF ST. THOMAS BECKET, BISHOP AND DOCTOR OF THE CHURCH

Heavenly Father, may we, led by the virtuous example of St. Thomas Becket, have the courage to live according to your holy will, even when that discipleship brings division, discord, and animosity. Draw the hearts of those far from you to convert and to bask in your divine love. We ask this in Jesus' name. Amen.

Feast of the Holy Family of Jesus, Mary, and Joseph (Sunday after Christmas)

O Holy Family of Jesus, Mary, and Joseph, may we be encouraged, inspired, and reliably enthused by the remarkable example that God provided in joining you together as a family. May our focus remain on the Lord Jesus Christ within the Holy Family; let us be as devoted to you, Lord, as Sts. Mary and Joseph were. In your name, we pray. Amen.

Epiphany

We give you thanks, Lord Jesus Christ, for having revealed yourself to humanity through the actions and words of the magi. Open our hearts to your presence and our eyes to your light, so that we may ever more joyfully bring others to an awareness of your goodness and your truth. Help us to reveal you to the nations as light and truth. And teach us to approach you with honor and awe as did those who came to know you here on earth, even from your infancy. Holy Lord, we humbly pray. Amen.

Feast of the Baptism of the Lord (Sunday after Epiphany)

Lord Jesus Christ, as the Christmas season draws to a close, encourage us to take seriously our baptismal promises in rejecting sin and making you known to the world by all we say and do. In your holy name, we pray. Amen.

FOR CHRISTMAS JOY THROUGHOUT THE YEAR

Lord Jesus, guide our hearts to celebrate your Incarnation not only during the Christmas season, but throughout the entire year. May we never tire of our devotion to you as the Christ Child. Likewise, may we never take for granted that you came into the world as an unborn child, and may we thus proclaim the sanctity of all human life, from the moment of conception until our natural death. We ask this in your name. Amen.

WINTER ORDINARY TIME

TO MAKE ORDINARY TIME EXTRAORDINARY

Lord God, with the Christmas season now concluded, let us continue to welcome you and your will into our lives during the first stretch of ordinary time this year. Let us recognize this time as an opportunity to accept the ways in which you *order* our lives and our thoughts. May this ordinary time become "extraordinary" as we acknowledge the central role that you play in our lives. Through Jesus Christ, we pray. Amen.

RECOGNIZING GOD IN THE EVERYDAY

Lord God, we recognize that you are all-powerful, all-knowing, and always with us. As we celebrate and contemplate the feast of the Presentation of the Lord during this winter, lead us to consider the mystery of your presence in our daily lives. Help us to fend off the temptation to keep these joyful reflections to ourselves; rather, may they be occasions for us to serve you faithfully and share through word and deed with all whom we meet the Good News of your coming to dwell among us. Amen.

LENT

AT THE BEGINNING OF LENT

Lord Jesus Christ, grant us a holy and purposeful Lenten season, as we purify our hearts through prayer, fasting, and almsgiving. May we fervently desire to welcome you into our lives by preparing our souls through the repentance of our sins, especially with the graces of the Sacrament of Reconciliation. May we always strive to live holier lives according to your divine will. In your holy name, we pray. Amen.

FOR ENCOURAGEMENT DURING LENT

Kind and merciful Lord, throughout this Lenten season, grant us your mercy, which we greatly desire. Be with us during this journey of spiritual preparation so that we can be bearers of your Good News to a world that is in such sorrowful need of your salvific redemption. May the prayer, fasting, and almsgiving of this Lent make our hearts ever purer in the interest of your will. We ask this in your divine name. Amen.

DURING HOLY WEEK AND TRIDUUM

Lord Jesus Christ, we are profoundly grateful to you for your Passion and Death, by which you achieved the expiation for our sins. During this Holy Week and Triduum, draw this parish community to meditate on the grand sacrifice that you performed for us. Draw us, with solemn hearts and minds, ever closer to your merciful love. We ask this in your holy name. Amen.

EASTER TO PENTECOST

AT THE BEGINNING OF EASTER

Risen Lord, we thank you for rising to new life on that first Easter Sunday. Bless our parish community during this Easter season as we meditate on the ultimate cause for our joy, which is the prospect of our salvation and eternal life with you in heaven. Please draw us heavenward at the end of our earthly days. We pray this in your holy name as the Lord of Life. Amen.

FOR HOPE AT EASTER

Lord God of hope, we thank you for the opportunity to celebrate Christ's Resurrection during this Easter season. Draw us into the glories of Easter, let joy fill us to overflowing, and may *Alleluia* be the song ever on our lips. Open our hearts and our wills to the hope that stems only from Easter, as we joyfully await the fulfillment of all of your promises, the greatest of which is the hope of eternal life with you. Amen.

For a Joyous Easter

Lord Jesus Christ, we thank you for the gift of your life and for the sacrifice of your life, a sacrifice thankfully surpassed by your glorious Resurrection. Open our hearts to the unadulterated joy that comes at Easter, a joy that we as your disciples are called to bring into the world. Please inspire the members of this parish community to proclaim that joy throughout our lives. We ask this in your wondrous name. Amen.

Divine Mercy Sunday (Sunday after Easter Sunday)

Lord Jesus Christ, as we continue to celebrate the joy of your glorious Resurrection on that first Easter Sunday, teach us to abide in your merciful heart. Encourage us to steadily seek solace in you alone and to convert ourselves daily to your divine will. Both on Divine Mercy Sunday and beyond, draw us to imitate St. Faustina Kowalska and all those who have similarly furthered your holy Gospel. Amen.

Solemnity of the Ascension of the Lord (Ascension Thursday)

Lord Jesus Christ, we celebrate today your marvelous Ascension into heaven, to which your surviving disciples bore witness while they were still enlivened by the joy of your Resurrection at Easter. Watch over the members of this community, inspiring in us opportunities to proclaim your glorious Ascension into heaven, when you took your throne at the right hand of the

Father. We ask this in the name of the Father, and of the Son, and of the Holy Spirit. Amen.

PENTECOST SUNDAY

We give thanks to you, Triune God, on this celebration of Pentecost. We implore the Holy Spirit to continue to enliven the members of this community, inspiring us to take seriously our call to apostolic zeal just as the apostles were inspired to evangelize zealously and fearlessly following Pentecost, the "birthday" of the Church. We thank you, loving God, for the opportunity to participate in the spiritually rewarding goal of spreading the Good News of Jesus Christ everywhere we go. In the same Christ, we pray. Amen.

SUMMER/FALL ORDINARY TIME

SOLEMNITY OF THE MOST HOLY TRINITY (FIRST SUNDAY AFTER PENTECOST)

Lord God, one God in three divine Persons, watch over this parish community on this joyous occasion of the Solemnity of the Most Holy Trinity. May we always endeavor to follow your divine will, living the Gospel charitably, zealously, and courageously. Remain with us throughout our lives, leading us heavenward by your profound desire to save us, especially from ourselves. We ask this in the holy name of the Father, and of the Son, and of the Holy Spirit. Amen.

Solemnity of the Most Holy Body and Blood of Christ or Corpus Christi (Second Sunday after Pentecost)

We give you thanks, Lord Jesus Christ, for your supreme sacrifice on the Cross. We likewise praise and thank you for having given us the fullness of yourself in gifts of bread and wine. Teach us to know you in the Eucharist and to seek your presence in one another and others we meet. May your Body and Blood bring us ever nearer to our eternal home with you in glory. We ask this in the power of the Holy Spirit. Amen.

Solemnity of the Most Sacred Heart of Jesus (Nineteen Days after Pentecost)

Lord Jesus Christ, on this Solemnity of your Most Sacred Heart, draw us into a deeper devotion to discipleship so that we can more faithfully both honor your Sacred Heart and seek shelter in it. May your Sacred Heart protect all of the members of this community so that through our devotion to you we may more effectively undertake our ministerial endeavors in service to your Good News. We ask this through your holy and divine name. Amen.

For Inspiration during Ordinary Time

Heavenly Father, please guide and draw us to look at Ordinary Time as an opportunity to grow ever closer to you. Fend off our tendency to view ordinary time as a boring, paltry, or banal period of the liturgical year. Let us find inspiration in the holy lives of the many saints of this era and imitate them in discipleship, all for your greater glory. We ask this in Christ's precious name. Amen.

AUGUST 15: SOLEMNITY OF THE ASSUMPTION OF THE BLESSED VIRGIN MARY

Mother Mary, as we celebrate your Assumption into heaven, remember us to your Son, the Lord Jesus Christ. May we be inspired by your virtuous devotion to the Lord God as we, too, seek to proclaim the wonders of the Good News to a world so fraught with doubt and unbelief. We ask this through your Son Jesus Christ. Amen.

OCTOBER 31: ALL HALLOWS' EVE

Heavenly Father, grant safety to those who are trick-or-treating or attending Halloween parties today. May the fun and festivities kindle in us a joy and wonder at your good creation. Draw your disciples—especially our young people—to look beyond today's playful activities toward the celebration of All Saints' Day tomorrow. Open our hearts to be inspired by the faithful witness of the holy men and women who have achieved eternal rest and are in our heavenly home, resting in your presence forever. Amen.

REMEMBERING THE DEAD DURING NOVEMBER

Merciful Father, we come to you today asking that you receive into paradise those souls who are in purgatory. Grant them entry into your eternal presence so that they may glorify your holy and wondrous name on earth. Amen.

LAST SUNDAY IN ORDINARY TIME: SOLEMNITY OF OUR LORD JESUS CHRIST, KING OF THE UNIVERSE

Lord Jesus Christ, King of the Universe, we admit that we do not always appreciate all that you have done for us throughout our lives. Draw us to recognize and celebrate you as the king of all that has ever been, is now, and will be. We pray this through your glorious and righteous name. Amen.

3.

Major Feasts, Solemnities, and Memorials by Month

JANUARY 1: SOLEMNITY OF MARY, THE HOLY MOTHER OF GOD

Mother Mary, please intercede for the members of this parish community. Ask your Son, the Lord Jesus Christ, our brother, to remain with us. May we always imitate your discipleship and love for the Lord, since you are the model devotee of the Lord God, in whose Incarnation you participated. We ask this in Jesus' name. Amen.

January 2: Memorial of Sts. Basil the Great and Gregory Nazianzen, Bishops and Doctors of the Church

Heavenly Father, guide the members of this parish to be inspired by the holy example of Sts. Basil the Great and Gregory Nazianzen, who courageously defended the truth of your goodness and providence. May we have their same zeal when it comes to evangelizing and living according to your holy will. In Jesus' name, we pray. Amen.

January 4: Memorial of St. Elizabeth Ann Seton, Religious

Holy Elizabeth Ann Seton, you loved children and brought them up according to the Catholic faith through the ministry of Catholic education. Ask the Lord to watch over all catechists and those involved in teaching the faith here in our parish community. We ask this in the name of Jesus the Lord. Amen.

January 5: Memorial of St. John Neumann, Bishop

St. John Neumann, please ask the Lord to intercede for all of the members of this parish community. May your holy example encourage and inspire both those in Catholic education and the Church's bishops to take their roles seriously. We ask this through Jesus Christ the Lord. Amen.

JANUARY 6: MEMORIAL OF ST. ANDRÉ BESSETTE, RELIGIOUS

Gracious Lord, draw us to look to the example of humility, faith, and devotion to the Gospel found in St. André Bessette. St. André had a deep devotion to St. Joseph; may we likewise act with a humble discipleship as we look for opportunities to promote your divine kingdom. In the name of Jesus, we pray. Amen.

JANUARY 17: MEMORIAL OF ST. ANTHONY, ABBOT

Lord God, we sometimes feel that life is filled with deserts. Yet it is often in those deserts that we are drawn closer to you and gain clarity about your will for us. May St. Anthony the Abbot, who entered the seclusion of the desert in order to grow closer to you, inspire us to find the oasis of your love. In Jesus' name, we pray. Amen.

JANUARY 20: MEMORIAL OF BL. BASIL MOREAU, PRIEST

Bl. Basil Moreau, you founded the Congregation of Holy Cross to bring the light of Christ into the spiritual darkness of post-revolutionary France; intercede for us so that we may more faithfully proclaim the Good News to a society in such need of the light of Christ. We pray this through the same Christ the Lord. Amen.

JANUARY 21: MEMORIAL OF ST. AGNES, VIRGIN AND MARTYR

Holy St. Agnes, you were a but a youth when you gave your life rather than deny your beliefs. May your example of holiness inspire the members of this parish community to promote fidelity to our beliefs. We ask this in the name of the Lord Jesus Christ. Amen.

JANUARY 22: DAY OF PRAYER FOR THE LEGAL PROTECTION OF UNBORN CHILDREN

We pray, Lord God, that you may place your protective hand on all unborn human lives. Please instill in mothers and fathers the courage to be good and loving to their children. Inspire throughout society a profound respect for all human life, beginning at the moment of conception. Help our lawmakers adopt this truth. Amen.

JANUARY 23: MEMORIAL OF ST. MARIANNE COPE, VIRGIN

Heavenly Father, may we look to the example of St. Marianne Cope when it comes to serving those living on the margins of society, especially through the ministry of Catholic education. May all catechists look to her example to invite others more faithfully to your loving heart. We ask this through Christ the Lord. Amen.

JANUARY 24: MEMORIAL OF ST. FRANCIS DE SALES, BISHOP AND DOCTOR OF THE CHURCH

Holy St. Francis de Sales, just as in your era, it can be a challenge today to remember that we are all called to holiness and that virtuous living is not expected only of a select few. Please intercede for this parish so that we may live faithfully according to Christian principles. We ask this in Christ's holy name. Amen.

JANUARY 25: FEAST OF THE CONVERSION OF ST. PAUL THE APOSTLE

Holy Apostle Paul, yours was probably the most famous conversion in the history of the Church. Intercede for this parish community so that we will be steadily transformed to magnify the Lord and his glory. Ask the Lord to change those whose hearts have been hardened. We ask this in Christ's holy, merciful name. Amen.

JANUARY 26: MEMORIAL OF STS. TIMOTHY AND TITUS, BISHOPS

Lord Jesus Christ, teach us to look to the example of Sts. Timothy and Titus, who accompanied your apostle Paul as he led missionary endeavors to spread your Gospel. May this community be inspired to invite and encourage one another to participate in the work of evangelization. We ask this in your holy name. Amen.

JANUARY 28: MEMORIAL OF ST. THOMAS AQUINAS, PRIEST AND DOCTOR OF THE CHURCH

Dear St. Thomas Aquinas, it was through your rich intellect and richer humility that you drew many souls to Christ. May we follow your example and open our minds and hearts to the Lord so that he can do his good work in us. Good St. Thomas, please intercede for those in the ministry of Catholic education and catechesis. We ask this through Christ the Lord. Amen.

FEBRUARY

FEBRUARY 2: PRESENTATION OF THE LORD OR CANDLEMAS

O God, true light of the heavens and the earth, on this the fortieth day after Christmas, let shine in us the power of your love. When the child Jesus was presented in the Temple to fulfill the Jewish law, he was also revealed to be our Lord and Savior. May we bring the light of that same Lord Jesus Christ to all whom we meet today and every day. Bless us, Lord God, with the power of your Holy Spirit and show us the way to the fullness of your kingdom. O, Light of Nations, come dwell in us anew. Amen.

FEBRUARY 5: MEMORIAL OF ST. AGATHA, VIRGIN AND MARTYR

Holy St. Agatha, at a young age, you bore witness to the Gospel, ultimately giving your life rather than deny the Lord Jesus

Christ. Please intercede for young people within this community and beyond, encouraging both them and adults to work for the benefit of the kingdom of God. We ask this through Christ's holy name. Amen.

FEBRUARY 6: MEMORIAL OF ST. PAUL MIKI AND COMPANIONS, MARTYRS

Lord God, as we celebrate the lives of St. Paul Miki and his companions, let us look for opportunities to similarly promote the Gospel with courage, conviction, zeal, and ultimately with love for you and our neighbor. May they intercede for us so that we can better serve your kingdom. We ask this through Christ the Lord. Amen.

FEBRUARY 8: MEMORIAL OF ST. JOSEPHINE BAKHITA, VIRGIN

St. Bakhita, we look to your example of holiness, which you maintained through harsh persecution. Intercede for the members of this community so that we may imitate your perseverance in the virtuous life. We ask this through Jesus Christ the Lord. Amen.

FEBRUARY 14: MEMORIAL OF STS. CYRIL, MONK, AND METHODIUS, BISHOP

Lord God, we may not all be called to travel abroad in order to bring the Good News of Jesus Christ to faraway lands. Nonetheless, may we be inspired by the example of Sts. Cyril and Methodius when it comes to seeking opportunities to spread your Word in the midst of demanding situations. We pray this in Christ the Lord. Amen.

FEBRUARY 14: MEMORIAL OF ST. VALENTINE, MARTYR

Lord Jesus Christ, inspire and encourage us by the example of St. Valentine to live according to your plan for chaste love. May those men and women who are called to marriage live faithfully, looking to the Holy Family as a model of virtue. We ask this in the name of Christ the Lord. Amen.

FEBRUARY 22: FEAST OF THE CHAIR OF ST. PETER THE APOSTLE

Holy apostle Peter, please intercede for this community. Ask the Lord to watch over his Church, led by Pope [pope's name], so that in his role as Vicar of Christ he may lead well the flock of your disciples here on earth, especially during difficult times. We ask this in the name of Jesus Christ, the Good Shepherd. Amen.

FEBRUARY 23: MEMORIAL OF ST. POLYCARP, BISHOP AND MARTYR

Lord God, encourage your faithful to look to the example of St. Polycarp when it comes to professing the truths of the Gospel, whether convenient or inconvenient. May we always look for opportunities to evangelize, thus drawing others to the prospect of the Beatific Vision. We ask this through Jesus Christ. Amen.

MARCH

MARCH 3: MEMORIAL OF ST. KATHARINE DREXEL, VIRGIN

St. Katharine Drexel, you devoted your life to serving and educating those living on the margins of society, especially the poor, children, and underserved ethnic minorities. Please help us bring the Gospel to all the marginalized in our communities, that they may know the Lord's preferential love for them. We ask this through the same Lord Jesus Christ. Amen.

MARCH 7: MEMORIAL OF STS. PERPETUA AND FELICITY, MARTYRS

Lord, our God, as we join in celebration of the sanctified lives of Sts. Perpetua and Felicity, may we imitate their devotion to you and their courage in advancing the Good News of Jesus Christ. May the Holy Spirit guide us in our desire to live according to your will, come what may. We ask this in the name of Jesus Christ the Lord. Amen.

MARCH 17: MEMORIAL OF ST. PATRICK, BISHOP

St. Patrick, you were instrumental in bringing the Gospel to Ireland. Please intercede for us so that we may draw others to the loving embrace of Jesus Christ, whom you proclaimed in your role as bishop and missionary. We make this prayer through the same Christ the Lord. Amen.

MARCH 19: SOLEMNITY OF ST. JOSEPH, SPOUSE OF THE BLESSED VIRGIN MARY

Good St. Joseph, whom we refer to as the "Silent Saint," we are inspired by your example of protection and holiness. Please ask the Lord to watch over and protect this community. May we never tire of living according to your example as a devotee of the Infant Jesus. We make this prayer through the same Christ the Lord. Amen.

MARCH 24: MEMORIAL OF ST. ÓSCAR ROMERO, BISHOP AND MARTYR

Lord God, be with us as we celebrate the life and legacy of St. Óscar Romero. Help us to speak up for those who have been marginalized in society, especially the poor and otherwise vulnerable. Inspire us to live as courageous witnesses of faith so that the world can know your love. We pray through Christ the Lord. Amen.

MARCH 25: SOLEMNITY OF THE ANNUNCIATION OF THE LORD

Lord Jesus Christ, draw us to yourself in celebration of the announcement that you entered the world. The archangel Gabriel proclaimed your entry and the Blessed Virgin Mary, your mother, accepted God's will. Let us likewise always say yes to your expectations that we proclaim the Gospel. We ask this in your name. Amen.

APRIL

APRIL 7: MEMORIAL OF ST. JOHN BAPTIST DE LA SALLE, PRIEST

Heavenly Father, evangelization can sometimes be challenging. Just as your servant St. John Baptist de la Salle made the Good News of Jesus Christ known through the ministry of Catholic education, may we within this community labor joyously to draw others to you. In Jesus' name, we pray. Amen.

APRIL 25: MEMORIAL OF ST. MARK THE EVANGELIST

Holy St. Mark, we thank you for giving us knowledge of Jesus Christ through your Gospel. Please intercede for us so that we can be inspired to evangelize using the unique gifts that God has given to us. We ask this through Jesus Christ, Lord, Savior, and Redeemer. Amen.

APRIL 29: MEMORIAL OF ST. CATHERINE OF SIENA, VIRGIN AND DOCTOR OF THE CHURCH

Lord Jesus Christ, your devotee St. Catherine of Siena ardently desired to encourage others to holiness, especially through repentance of sin and the unity of the Church. May we, especially those of us who are similarly within the laity, look to St. Catherine's example of virtue in all that we do. We ask this in your holy name. Amen.

MAY

MAY 2: MEMORIAL OF ST. ATHANASIUS, BISHOP AND DOCTOR OF THE CHURCH

Heavenly Father, please draw us to be inspired by the life of St. Athanasius, who loved you deeply and therefore proclaimed your truth despite the odds against him. Please inspire in us a profound devotion to the sacred scriptures and help us share the joys of discipleship. We ask this in Jesus' name. Amen.

MAY 3: MEMORIAL OF STS. PHILIP AND JAMES, APOSTLES

Lord God, we give you thanks for the holy lives of Sts. Philip and James. Just as they followed your Son Jesus Christ faithfully during his earthly ministry, may we pursue opportunities to evangelize and draw others to Christ's embrace. We make this prayer through the same Christ our Lord. Amen.

MAY 10: MEMORIAL OF ST. DAMIEN DE VEUSTER (MOLOKAI), PRIEST

Holy St. Damien, we are grateful for your life and your example of serving these sick with leprosy, who were ostracized because others so feared them. Please help us also see the face of Christ in others, no matter their situation, circumstance, or condition. We ask this through the same Jesus Christ. Amen.

MAY 14: FEAST OF ST. MATTHIAS, APOSTLE

Lord Jesus Christ, we give thanks for the apostolic zeal of your holy witness St. Matthias. May he intercede for us as we imitate his example of discipleship and community, striving to help others during their journeys to you. May we be similarly inspired to go out and proclaim your Good News at every opportunity. Amen.

MAY 15: MEMORIAL OF ST. ISIDORE

Creator God, watch over the members of this community as we strive to appreciate the wonders of the natural world that you have given us. St. Isidore drew others to value nature; may we never cease to be impressed by the glories of your creation. We pray this in the name of Jesus Christ the Lord. Amen.

MAY 26: MEMORIAL OF ST. PHILIP NERI, PRIEST

Dear St. Philip, you were the friend of many and demonstrated a joyful Christian demeanor. Please ask the Lord to help us also exude the joy in Christ that you shared with everyone you encountered. We ask this through the same Christ the Lord. Amen.

MAY 29: MEMORIAL OF ST. PAUL VI, POPE

Heavenly Father, we are grateful for the life of your servant St. Paul VI, who dedicated his pontificate to fostering peace, unity, and holiness throughout society, even when he faced great challenges. May we imitate his example and so grow closer to Christ, in whose name we pray. Amen.

MAY 31: FEAST OF THE VISITATION OF THE BLESSED VIRGIN MARY

Dear Mother Mary, please intercede for us with your divine Son. Elizabeth and John the Baptist experienced profound joy in the presence of Christ as an unborn baby when you went to see them; help us bring the joy of Christ to all people we encounter. We pray this in Christ's holy name. Amen.

JUNE

JUNE 1: MEMORIAL OF ST. JUSTIN, MARTYR

Lord God, in every age, mixed and false messages lead people astray. Just as St. Justin surveyed the philosophical principles of his time and found your truth in their midst, may we also courageously profess the beauty of the Gospel. We ask this in Jesus' name. Amen.

JUNE 3: MEMORIAL OF STS. CHARLES LWANGA AND COMPANIONS, MARTYRS

Holy St. Charles Lwanga, you and your companions were only boys when your lives were brutally taken because you professed your faith in Jesus Christ. Please ask the Lord to protect our youth in a special way, guiding them to right principles and the incalculable joy that comes with discipleship. We ask this in Jesus' holy and righteous name. Amen.

June 5: Memorial of St. Boniface, Bishop and Martyr

Heavenly Father, we are grateful for the life of St. Boniface. May we look to him as an example of holiness and profound love for the truth of the Gospel. When we are challenged by difficulties and setbacks, may we keep our eyes on the Cross, aware that Jesus is ever present with us. We make this prayer through his divine name. Amen.

June 11: Memorial of St. Barnabas, Apostle

Holy St. Barnabas, please pray for this community, that the Lord to bring unity and agreement, in our work of evangelization. Please ask the Lord to watch over us so that we can find and practice new methods of spreading his Good News. We ask this through Christ the Lord. Amen.

June 13: Memorial of St. Anthony of Padua, Priest and Doctor of the Church

Lord God, St. Anthony of Padua had a rich intellect and a strong devotion to the Child Jesus; may we likewise use our spiritual gifts to bring the Gospel out into the world. Watch over this community, ensuring that we commit ourselves to a life of fervent discipleship. We pray this in Jesus' glorious name. Amen.

June 21: Memorial of St. Aloysius Gonzaga, Religious

St. Aloysius, you lived a life of piety, chastity, simplicity, and deep devotion to the Lord. Please intercede for the members of this community that we be drawn to imitate the Christian witness of your holiness. We pray this through the Lord Jesus Christ. Amen.

June 24: Solemnity of the Nativity of St. John the Baptist

St. John the Baptist, we give thanks to God for your exemplary role in bringing the light of Christ into the world. Please ask the Lord to watch over this community so that we can act with the same loving conviction that you maintained throughout your ministry. We make this prayer through Christ the Lord. Amen.

June 28: Memorial of St. Irenaeus, Bishop and Martyr

Dear God, draw our attention to the example of your holy servant St. Irenaeus. Just as he endeavored to introduce the correct teachings about Christ to a weary world against much opposition, may we persevere through the obstacles that we encounter in the spiritual life. We make this prayer in the holy name of Jesus the Lord. Amen.

June 29: Solemnity of Sts. Peter and Paul, Apostles

Holy Sts. Peter and Paul, despite your occasionally divergent personalities, you labored together to bring knowledge of Christ into the world in the decades after his public ministry. May we within this community also collaborate with fellow disciples in order to evangelize more effectively. We ask this in Jesus' name. Amen.

JULY

July 1: Memorial of St. Junípero Serra, Priest

O holy Junípero, evangelization can sometimes be a daunting task. You traveled tirelessly to spread the Gospel and perform missionary endeavors; please intercede for us that we may also use our time, talent, and treasure to bring others to the love of Jesus Christ. We ask this through the same Christ our Lord. Amen.

July 3: Feast of St. Thomas, Apostle

Lord Jesus Christ, inspire us to follow the Christian example of your holy apostle Thomas, who was the last to recognize you as the Risen Lord. May we readily recognize who you are and thus draw others to acknowledge your role as Messiah, Lord, Savior, Redeemer, and God Incarnate. We ask this in your holy name. Amen.

July 5: Memorial of St. Elizabeth of Portugal

Heavenly Father, may we look to the example of your faithful daughter St. Elizabeth of Portugal. Pour yourself into our hearts and inspire us to better serve those living in challenging situations and seemingly insurmountable circumstances. We pray this through Christ the Lord. Amen.

July 11: Memorial of St. Benedict, Abbot

Holy St. Benedict, you showed us how the bonds of a shared life can draw a community closer to the Lord. Please intercede for us within this community that we might commit ourselves to Christ and his Gospel in charity and dedication. We ask this through Christ the Lord. Amen.

July 14: Memorial of St. Kateri Tekakwitha, Virgin

Lord God, we thank you for the saintly life of your disciple St. Kateri Tekakwitha. May we look to her for inspiration to personal sanctity when we face others' disapproval. Through her intercession, may we be fearless disciples whose focus is on serving the kingdom of God. We make this prayer through Christ the Lord. Amen.

July 15: Memorial of St. Bonaventure, Bishop and Doctor of the Church

Holy St. Bonaventure, we implore your intercession today. You used your rich intellect to build up the kingdom of God; please ask the Lord to help us use our minds to serve him. Please intercede in a special way for all bishops as well. We make this prayer in Jesus' holy and righteous name. Amen.

July 18: Memorial of St. Camillus de Lellis, Priest

Father God, open our minds and hearts to imitate the virtuous example of St. Camillus. May we see your face when we encounter those living in poverty, the chronically ill, and the otherwise disadvantaged. May the Holy Spirit guide us to see them as cherished brothers and sisters. We make this prayer through Jesus Christ. Amen.

July 22: Memorial of St. Mary Magdalene

Lord Jesus Christ, of all of the people who followed you during your earthly ministry, Mary Magdalene was the first to witness you as the Risen Lord. May we exude confidence and joy as did St. Mary Magdalene when we share the truth of your victory over sin and death. We ask this in your holy name. Amen.

July 25: Feast of St. James, Apostle

Holy St. James the Apostle, you followed the Lord faithfully during his earthly ministry and gave your life sharing his Gospel. Please intercede for the members of this community that we may build up the kingdom of God. We pray this through Jesus the Lord. Amen.

July 26: Memorial of Sts. Joachim and Anne, Parents of the Blessed Virgin Mary

Lord Jesus Christ, on this day when we celebrate your maternal grandparents, watch over us in a special way. Please inspire all mothers and fathers, grandmothers and grandfathers, and other family members to serve the kingdom of God within their respective familial roles. We ask this in your holy name. Amen.

July 29: Memorial of St. Martha

Heavenly Father, let us recall the holy example of St. Martha. We can all get so busy and preoccupied with worldly worries that we forget what matters most: spending time with the Lord God. Please encourage us to make time to devote ourselves to resting in your divine presence. We make this prayer in Jesus' name. Amen.

July 31: Memorial of St. Ignatius of Loyola, Priest

Lord God, St. Ignatius of Loyola changed his life for the better by becoming your disciple and drawing others to labor for your greater glory. Please guide us to reflect on the magnitude of your wonderful goodness so that we also can better conform ourselves to your holy will. We pray this in Jesus' divine name. Amen.

AUGUST

AUGUST 1: MEMORIAL OF ST. ALPHONSUS LIGUORI, BISHOP AND DOCTOR OF THE CHURCH

Holy St. Alphonsus, it was through your holy example that many souls were brought to Christ by realizing how they were called to follow him using their time, talent, and treasure. Please intercede for this community that we likewise use our gifts to spread the Gospel and let Christ's light shine. Through the same Christ, we pray. Amen.

AUGUST 4: MEMORIAL OF ST. JOHN VIANNEY, PRIEST

Lord Jesus Christ, your servant St. John Vianney had such a strong devotion to you. His heart was on fire for you throughout his priesthood, and he brought many souls back to you, especially through the Sacrament of Reconciliation. May we look to his holy example, particularly as we pray for our parish priests. In your name, we pray. Amen.

AUGUST 6: FEAST OF THE TRANSFIGURATION OF THE LORD

Lord Jesus Christ, as we commemorate your display of your heavenly glory to the apostles Peter, James, and John, please draw us to always recognize and appreciate who you truly are: fully God and fully man. May we look for numerous opportunities to proclaim this truth to all mankind. In your holy name, we pray. Amen.

AUGUST 8: MEMORIAL OF ST. DOMINIC, PRIEST

Lord God, as we look at the pious and devout life of your servant St. Dominic, let us never shy away from the chance to
proclaim the beauty of the Gospel to a weary, confused world.
May we each preach the Good News in formative ways to both
current and future disciples. In Jesus' name, we pray. Amen.

AUGUST 10: FEAST OF ST. LAWRENCE, DEACON AND MARTYR

Heavenly Father, as worldly worries and distractions creep in,
it can be a real challenge for us to proclaim the fullness of
your goodness to humanity. May we have the same resolve and
commitment to the Gospel as St. Lawrence did, showing that
the true treasure of the Church is her members. In Jesus' holy
name, we pray. Amen.

AUGUST 11: MEMORIAL OF ST. CLARE OF ASSISI, VIRGIN

Holy Clare of Assisi, please intercede for this community today.
We here on earth are always in need of inspiration when it
comes to collaborating with fellow disciples in the interest of
furthering the Gospel. Therefore, we implore your intercession
that we be drawn to value and appreciate virtue as much as you
did. Amen.

August 15: Solemnity of the Assumption of the Blessed Virgin Mary

Dear Mother Mary, as we celebrate your Assumption into heaven, please pray for us to your Son, the Lord Jesus Christ. May we be inspired by your virtuous devotion to the Lord God as we, too, seek to proclaim the wonders of the Good News to a world so fraught with doubt and unbelief. We ask this through your Son Jesus Christ. Amen.

August 20: Memorial of St. Bernard of Clairvaux, Abbot and Doctor of the Church

Heavenly Father, we give thanks today for the holy example and intellectually enriching writings of your holy disciple St. Bernard of Clairvaux. Through his intercession, may we be encouraged to use the gifts of our hearts and minds to bring the Good News of Christ into society. We pray this through the same Lord Jesus. Amen.

August 21: Memorial of St. Pius X, Pope

Heavenly Father, as St. Pius X defended the orthodox teachings of the Church, may we also stand firm in our convictions and defend the faith in our often tumultuous world. Teach us to cling fast to the Gospel, to love neighbor as ourselves, to work for justice, and draw ever closer to your will and to the work of your kingdom every day of our lives. We ask this through the same Christ our Lord. Amen.

August 22: Memorial of the Queenship of the Blessed Virgin Mary

Mother Mary, Queen of the Universe, we come to you today to plead your intercession for us sinful humans. Please draw us to your Immaculate Heart and the Sacred Heart of Jesus, that we may be increasingly inspired to live lives of holy service to the kingdom of God. We ask this through your Son Jesus Christ. Amen.

August 23: Memorial of St. Rose of Lima, Virgin

Lord Jesus Christ, your holy servant St. Rose of Lima was devoted to you and your Good News throughout her life. May we have that same singular focus and purpose within our own lives so that we are steadily drawn to reflect on the wonders of your holy will. We ask this in your glorious and righteous name. Amen.

August 24: Feast of St. Bartholomew, Apostle

Good St. Bartholomew, we implore you to intercede for us to the Lord God. May we be inspired by your holy life never to waver in our discipleship, come what may. Please ask the Lord to grant us that same resolve and focus in our commitment to the kingdom of God. We ask this through Jesus Christ the Lord. Amen.

August 27: Memorial of St. Monica

Dear St. Monica, may we be drawn to imitate your exemplary patience and other virtues. You knew that your son, St.

Augustine of Hippo, would one day return to the Lord; please intercede for all of us, especially those whose children are astray from the will of Christ. We ask this through the same Christ the Lord. Amen.

AUGUST 28: MEMORIAL OF ST. AUGUSTINE OF HIPPO, BISHOP AND DOCTOR OF THE CHURCH

Heavenly Father, guide us to imitate the example of repentance and virtue shown in the life of your holy disciple St. Augustine of Hippo. Draw us to your heart like the Prodigal Son so that we can know the merciful embrace of your profound fatherly love for us. We ask this through the Lord Jesus Christ. Amen.

AUGUST 29: MEMORIAL OF THE PASSION OF ST. JOHN THE BAPTIST

Father God, it was St. John the Baptist who proclaimed the coming of your Son, the Lord Jesus Christ. Inspire us to have the same courage and devotion to the Good News that John the Baptist demonstrated, even when we are going against what is immoral but popularly accepted. We pray this in the name of Jesus the Lord. Amen.

SEPTEMBER

SEPTEMBER 3: MEMORIAL OF ST. GREGORY THE GREAT, POPE AND DOCTOR OF THE CHURCH

Spirit of God, through the intercession of St. Gregory, pour out your holy wisdom on those charged with leading your Church. Strengthen them in adversity; grant them clarity of mind and purity of desire. May they, like our Lord Jesus, empty themselves in loving service to the kingdom of God, the fulfillment of which we eagerly await. We pray in the name of Christ Jesus, our Lord. Amen.

SEPTEMBER 5: MEMORIAL OF ST. TERESA OF CALCUTTA, RELIGIOUS

Holy Mother Teresa of Calcutta, please intercede for us that we may see the Lord Jesus Christ in our neighbor, from the unborn child to the materially destitute and everyone in between. Even in the dark times of life, may we be drawn to imitate your example and remain devoted to seeking God's will. We pray this in Jesus' name. Amen.

SEPTEMBER 8: FEAST OF THE NATIVITY OF THE BLESSED VIRGIN MARY

Lord Jesus Christ, please watch over the members of this community as we celebrate the birth of your mother, the Blessed Virgin Mary. As your first disciple, she is our model of the Christian life, our queen, and our mother. May we follow

Mary's example of selfless virtue and moral righteousness in our desire to follow God's will. Guard us against despair by drawing us close to your mother in all we do. Through the intercession of Mary, we pray. Amen.

SEPTEMBER 9: MEMORIAL OF ST. PETER CLAVER, PRIEST

Good St. Peter Claver, you were devoted to drawing attention to the plight of those living in dire poverty and injustice. You raised these people up to recognize their inherent dignity; please intercede for us that we may be encouraged to work against modern-day slavery and human trafficking. In Christ's name, we pray. Amen.

SEPTEMBER 13: MEMORIAL OF ST. JOHN CHRYSOSTOM, BISHOP AND DOCTOR OF THE CHURCH

Holy St. John Chrysostom, you employed your rich intellect and model piety to draw many souls to the Lord Jesus Christ. Please ask the Lord to protect the members of this community and help us to find new and effective ways of bringing souls to Christ. We ask this through the same Jesus Christ the Lord. Amen.

SEPTEMBER 14: FEAST OF THE EXALTATION OF THE HOLY CROSS

Lord Jesus Christ, you bore your Cross for us, giving that which we could not give in order to rescue our sinful souls from eternal condemnation. Inspire us never to take your sacrifice for granted, but to lift up our own daily crosses, attaching them to your salvific Passion, Death, and Resurrection. We ask this in your holy name. Amen.

SEPTEMBER 15: MEMORIAL OF OUR LADY OF SORROWS

Heavenly Father, as we honor today the Blessed Virgin Mary, encourage us to imitate her in our discipleship, in order to make us more faithful followers of your Son's Gospel. Draw us to always remember what Mary endured spiritually as she watched her Son suffer, inspiring us to likewise remain faithful. Amen.

SEPTEMBER 16: MEMORIAL OF STS. CORNELIUS, POPE, AND CYPRIAN, BISHOP, MARTYRS

Lord Jesus Christ, we thank you for the lives of Sts. Cornelius and Cyprian, who gave of themselves to the point of death in order to proclaim your Good News to a world in need of your promises. Please draw the members of this community to imitate their devotedness. In your name, we pray. Amen.

SEPTEMBER 20: MEMORIAL OF STS. ANDREW KIM TAE-GŎN, PRIEST, AND PAUL CHŎNG HA-SANG, AND COMPANIONS, MARTYRS

Lord, our God, we give thanks today for the holy lives and courageous witness of Sts. Andrew Kim Tae-gŏn, Paul Chŏng Ha-sang, and their companions. May we look to their example of fruitful holiness, endeavoring to bring your Good News to a wounded world that can only be healed by your love. In Jesus' holy name, we pray. Amen.

September 21: Feast of St. Matthew, Apostle and Evangelist

Lord Jesus Christ, your apostle and evangelist St. Matthew helps us recognize that it was you alone who fulfilled the messianic prophecies. May we be inspired to use our awareness of the gospels to introduce others to the wonders of your holy name, in which we pray. Amen.

September 23: Memorial of St. Pius of Pietrelcina ("Padre Pio"), Priest

Virtuous St. Padre Pio, please intercede for us to encourage us in our spiritual journeys, which you mastered so well during your earthly life. May we imitate your example of fidelity to the Gospel, and thereby draw others to know the eternal rewards that come with following Jesus Christ, in whose name we pray. Amen.

September 27: Memorial of St. Vincent de Paul, Priest

Lord Jesus Christ, your faithful disciple St. Vincent de Paul drew many to your merciful love by recognizing in others— especially those living in both material and spiritual poverty— your holy face. May we imitate his virtue and thus walk with you more faithfully. In your name, we pray. Amen.

September 29: Feast of Sts. Michael, Gabriel, and Raphael, Archangels

Holy archangels, we know from the sacred scriptures that it your divine messages help humanity know and more faithfully follow God's will. Pray for us that we may just as faithfully serve as disciples of the Lord Jesus Christ, in whose holy and righteous name we pray. Amen.

September 30: Memorial of St. Jerome, Priest and Doctor of the Church

Holy St. Jerome, you made the sacred scriptures available to many more people. We ask you pray for us that God may open our minds and hearts to receiving his Holy Word. We ask this in Jesus' name. Amen.

OCTOBER

October 1: Memorial of St. Thérèse of the Child Jesus, Virgin and Doctor of the Church

Lord Jesus Christ, our spiritual lives can be filled with times of consolation and difficulty. May we look to the life of St. Thérèse of Lisieux as inspiration because she brought so many to fathom the depths of your love. Help us to strengthen our devotion to your Gospel so that we, too, may feel your love in good times and bad. In your sacred name, we pray. Amen.

October 2: Memorial of the Holy Guardian Angels

Holy guardian angels, especially our individual guardian angels, we ask that you bring our petitions to the Lord God on his heavenly throne. When we are awake and when we are asleep, please guard and protect us through your intercession and guide us on the path to eternal life with Jesus the Lord. In the same Christ, we pray. Amen.

October 4: Memorial of St. Francis of Assisi

Heavenly Father, please draw us to imitate the faithful and pious example of your son and servant St. Francis of Assisi. May we similarly serve those who are mired in spiritual and material poverty, thereby serving your Son Jesus Christ. We pray this through the same Christ the Lord. Amen.

October 5: Memorial of Bl. Francis Xavier Seelos, Priest

Lord God, we give thanks today for the holy life of St. Francis Xavier Seelos, whose legacy has brought knowledge of the Gospel to so many generations through the ministry of Catholic education. May we imitate his example by evangelizing to the youth and inspiring them to do likewise. We ask this in Jesus' name. Amen.

OCTOBER 6: MEMORIAL OF BL. MARIE ROSE DUROCHER

Dear Bl. Marie Rose Durocher, please intercede for the members of this community so that we may imitate your holiness and inspire others to develop a personal relationship with Jesus Christ, including through the ministerial endeavors of Catholic education. We pray this in Jesus' name. Amen.

OCTOBER 7: MEMORIAL OF OUR LADY OF THE ROSARY

Blessed Virgin Mary, our Queen and Mother, please bring our prayers to your Son, the Lord Jesus Christ. As we meditate on the Mysteries of the Holy Rosary, may we be drawn increasingly to reflect on the eternal benefits of living according to Christ's promises. We make this prayer in Jesus' holy name. Amen.

OCTOBER 11: MEMORIAL OF ST. JOHN XXIII, POPE

Dear Lord Jesus Christ, we offer our prayers to you in gratitude for the virtuous life of your servant St. John XXIII. Help us, especially those in the Church's hierarchy, live more faithfully the Good News that you have given to humanity. In your glorious name, we pray. Amen.

OCTOBER 15: MEMORIAL OF ST. TERESA OF JESUS, VIRGIN AND DOCTOR OF THE CHURCH

Lord God, draw us to the same fidelity shown by your pious servant St. Teresa, that we may more effectively invite others into an understanding of the need for deeper and more fervent prayer. May those prayers draw us into a true relationship with your Son Jesus Christ, in whose name we pray. Amen.

OCTOBER 17: MEMORIAL OF ST. IGNATIUS OF ANTIOCH, BISHOP AND MARTYR

Heavenly Father, St. Ignatius of Antioch introduced some words that we as a Church now take for granted—such as the terms *Catholic* and *Eucharist*—only decades into Church history. May we imitate his selfless example of living according to the Gospel of Jesus Christ, in whose name we pray. Amen.

OCTOBER 18: FEAST OF ST. LUKE, EVANGELIST

Lord Jesus Christ, we give thanks today for the life of your holy servant St. Luke, whose gospel gives us a special awareness of your early years. May we, too, share your Good News with others accurately and lovingly. We make this prayer in your holy name. Amen.

OCTOBER 19: MEMORIAL OF STS. JEAN DE BRÉBEUF, ISAAC JOGUES, AND COMPANIONS, MARTYRS

Dear courageous Sts. Jean de Brébeuf, Isaac Jogues, and your companions, we ask for your powerful intercession today. Please intercede for us that we may be both zealous and charitable in sharing Christ's Good News with others. We ask this through the same Jesus Christ the Lord. Amen.

OCTOBER 20: MEMORIAL OF ST. PAUL OF THE CROSS, PRIEST

Dear Lord Jesus Christ, on this memorial of St. Paul of the Cross, draw us to a better respect, appreciation, and love for the sacrifice you offered on that dark Friday afternoon. Let us follow the example of St. Paul of the Cross to enter into a deeper relationship with you. In your name, we pray. Amen.

OCTOBER 22: MEMORIAL OF ST. JOHN PAUL II, POPE

Lord God, today we thank you for the faithful example of your virtuous disciple St. John Paul II, who spent his life interacting with people of all segments of society in service to the Gospel. As we imitate his virtue, please inspire us to use our time and energy spreading the Good News of Christ, in whose name we pray. Amen.

OCTOBER 28: FEAST OF STS. SIMON AND JUDE, APOSTLES

Heavenly Father, we thank you for the lives of Sts. Simon and Jude, apostles of your Son Jesus Christ, who dedicated their last years to following the Lord and spreading his Gospel, all the way to the point of martyrdom. May we imitate their courageous witness. We ask this through Christ the Lord. Amen.

NOVEMBER

NOVEMBER 1: FEAST OF ALL SAINTS

Lord in heaven above, we celebrate today all the saints who have reached the fullness of eternal life with you because of their faithfulness. Fashion our minds and hearts to also follow the Good News of Jesus Christ throughout the remainder of our days. May the saints in heaven guard and guide us. May the angels lead us home at the end of our earthly lives so that we may join the saints and you, our Lord and King, in the glory of heaven. We pray in your holy name. Amen.

NOVEMBER 2: FEAST OF ALL SOULS

Dear Lord God, we come to you today to plead that you receive into your eternal presence the souls of those who have gone before us. Grant your clement mercy to those souls currently experiencing purification in purgatory so that they may thereafter intercede for us who are currently earthbound. We ask this in Christ's sanctifying name. Amen.

NOVEMBER 3: MEMORIAL OF ST. MARTÍN DE PORRES, RELIGIOUS

Lord Jesus Christ, your holy servant St. Martín de Porres was faithfully devoted to you in light of his baptismal promises. May he intercede for us today to foster peace, goodwill, and charity between all of us, especially in communities with people of different ethnic backgrounds. We make this prayer in your holy name. Amen.

November 4: Memorial of St. Charles Borromeo, Bishop

Heavenly Father, we express our gratitude for the saintly model we find in St. Charles Borromeo. Inspire us to serve with fidelity those living in material and spiritual poverty, and encourage all of your bishops and other priests to be holy men living to zealously spread the Gospel. We ask this in the name of Jesus the Lord. Amen.

November 9: Feast of the Dedication of the Lateran Basilica

Lord Jesus Christ, we give thanks today for the Catholic Church that you founded upon the See of Peter. Watch over the Church, and allow her to bring your Good News into the world just as the early Church did so many epochs ago. We make this prayer in your holy name. Amen.

November 10: Memorial of St. Leo the Great, Pope and Doctor of the Church

We give thanks, Lord in heaven, for the holy life of St. Leo the Great. Encourage us to imitate his example of piety, humility, and fortitude in order to foster unity and positive accord in an occasionally divided Church. We pray this asking for the intercession of St. Leo the Great. Amen.

NOVEMBER 11: MEMORIAL OF ST. MARTIN OF TOURS, BISHOP

Dear Lord God, draw us to fashion our lives after the example of your holy servant St. Martin of Tours. Like Martin, may we proclaim the Gospel devotedly and fearlessly, even when it is met with opposition from a world that needs Jesus' Good News more than it may realize. We pray this through the same Christ the Lord. Amen.

NOVEMBER 12: MEMORIAL OF ST. JOSAPHAT, BISHOP AND MARTYR

Holy St. Josaphat, we implore your intercession for this community today. Please pray that unity, peace, goodwill, and charity may reign in society and in the Church, especially amid division and discord. We ask this prayer through the Lord Jesus Christ. Amen.

NOVEMBER 13: MEMORIAL OF ST. FRANCES XAVIER CABRINI, VIRGIN

Almighty Father in heaven, we pray to you in gratitude for the saintly life of your servant Frances Xavier Cabrini, who performed such marvelous ministry in service to the Church through the apostolate of Catholic education. Encourage all Catholic educators to imitate her example. In Christ's name, we pray. Amen.

NOVEMBER 15: MEMORIAL OF ST. ALBERT THE GREAT, BISHOP AND DOCTOR OF THE CHURCH

Lord Jesus Christ, lead and guide us to use our intellects and hearts to serve the kingdom of God and spread your Gospel, as did your devotee St. Albert the Great. May we never hesitate to use our gifts to bring other souls to your merciful heart. We ask this in your holy name. Amen.

NOVEMBER 16: MEMORIAL OF ST. MARGARET OF SCOTLAND

Dear Lord God, it is frequently difficult for us to discern what you are calling us to do. Through the intercession of St. Margaret of Scotland, may we have the spiritual clarity to follow your will and discover how we can best live in service to the Gospel of Jesus Christ, in whose glorious name we pray. Amen.

NOVEMBER 17: MEMORIAL OF ST. ELIZABETH OF HUNGARY, RELIGIOUS

Lord Jesus Christ, our kingly brother, it is often challenging for us to take our status as royalty—given at Baptism—seriously. May we be inspired to imitate your servant, St. Elizabeth of Hungary, to use our time, talent, and treasure to serve our neighbors, all in the interest of your Good News. In your name, we pray. Amen.

November 18: Memorial of St. Rose Philippine Duchesne, Virgin

Heavenly Father, we offer to you this day our gratitude for the exemplary life of your servant St. Rose Philippine Duchesne. Rose helped share the Gospel to those living in faraway places; may we follow her saintly example of evangelization. We ask this in the name of Jesus Christ the Lord. Amen.

November 21: Memorial of the Presentation of the Blessed Virgin Mary

Dear Mother Mary, please intercede for us in a special way today as we celebrate your presentation in the Temple by your parents, Sts. Joachim and Anne. We implore you to ask your Son, the Lord Jesus Christ, to watch over this community so that we can be effectively strengthened to share his Good News with everyone whom we meet. Amen.

November 22: Memorial of St. Cecilia, Virgin and Martyr

Dear Lord God, we are particularly grateful today for the saintly life of your servant St. Cecilia. As the patroness of musicians and musical ministries, may she intercede for all of our parish's musicians. May the faithful with musical talents be inspired by her courage and fortitude and may they serve with joy this parish community. Amen.

NOVEMBER 23: MEMORIAL OF BL. MIGUEL AGUSTÍN PRO, PRIEST AND MARTYR

We are ever grateful, Lord God, for your faithful disciples who have been devoted to you to the point of offering their earthly lives as a witness to your Gospel. May we be inspired by your servant Bl. Miguel Agustín Pro to have the same fortitude. In the name of Jesus, we pray. Amen.

NOVEMBER 24: MEMORIAL OF STS. ANDREW DŨNG-LẠC, PRIEST, AND COMPANIONS, MARTYRS

Heavenly Father, we express our gratitude now for the holy lives of your servants Sts. Andrew Dũng-Lạc and his companions, all of whom gave their lives for the sake of the Gospel. Embolden this community to more effectively and courageously spread the same Good News. In Jesus' name, we pray. Amen.

NOVEMBER 25: MEMORIAL OF ST. CATHERINE OF ALEXANDRIA, VIRGIN AND MARTYR

Lord God in heaven, your servant St. Catherine of Alexandria was only an adolescent when she spoke up against the injustices that the Roman Empire was inflicting upon Holy Mother Church and gave her life as a result. Encourage us to live the Gospel with conviction and charity. We pray this in Jesus' name. Amen.

November 30: Feast of St. Andrew, Apostle

Lord Jesus Christ, please draw us to follow the holy example of your apostle Andrew, the first disciple whom you chose. Just as St. Andrew brought your Good News to distant areas in the decades after your public ministry, may we, too, be inspired to evangelize with courage and boundless energy. In your holy name, we pray. Amen.

DECEMBER

December 3: Memorial of St. Francis Xavier, Priest

Heavenly Lord, we give thanks today for the evangelical model shown by your servant St. Francis Xavier. Enthused by his example and his intercession, may we endeavor to bring the Gospel to those both nearby and in faraway lands. We ask this through the Lord Jesus Christ, sovereign of the global Catholic Church. Amen.

December 6: Memorial of St. Nicholas, Bishop

Lord God, we are especially grateful today for the saintly life of Nicholas, who served your Son Jesus Christ faithfully in his ministries. St. Nicholas used his role as bishop to aid those in both spiritual and material poverty; may we also spread the Gospel and draw others to the loving demands of Christian love. Teach us the joy of giving and as we continue to prepare for Christmas. In the spirit of Nicholas, we pray. Amen.

December 7: Memorial of St. Ambrose, Bishop and Doctor of the Church

Heavenly Father, we come to you grateful for the holy example of St. Ambrose of Milan, who labored within his ministry as bishop for the unity of the Church and to draw others into lives of holiness. Through his intercession, may we strive to live more in accord with Christ's holy Gospel. We ask this in Jesus' name. Amen.

December 8: Solemnity of the Immaculate Conception of the Blessed Virgin Mary

All loving God, we give you thanks this day for our Blessed Mother, conceived without sin and our most holy example of the Christian life. May we, like Mary, open our lives to your divine will and may Christ be born again in us as we prepare for the coming of Christmas. Amen.

December 9: Memorial of St. Juan Diego Cuauhtlatoatzin

Heavenly Father, we thank you for the holy example of St. Juan Diego, who devotedly cooperated with Our Lady of Guadalupe to spread the Good News of Jesus Christ to the people of Mexico. Bless with courage the members of this community as we endeavor to imitate St. Juan's virtue and humility. Amen.

December 12: Feast of Our Lady of Guadalupe

Lord God above, we give thanks to you for the life of Mother Mary, who provided an example of piety, selflessness, and grace during her time on earth. May we continue to look to her under the title *Our Lady of Guadalupe* as an example of virtue. We pray through her intercession for the Church both in the Americas and around the globe. May the Virgin of Guadalupe be a guiding light even in our darkest days. Amen.

December 13: Memorial of St. Lucy, Virgin and Martyr

Lord Jesus Christ, we are grateful for the zealous witness of St. Lucy, a young woman who served those in both material and spiritual poverty during the Roman Empire's persecution of the early Church. May we be drawn to imitate her courageous charity. In your name, we pray. Amen.

December 14: Memorial of St. John of the Cross, Priest and Doctor of the Church

Heavenly Father, your holy servant St. John remained steadfast as he endured persecution and imprisonment for his efforts at reforming the Church. May his patient example of devotion to you in the darkness of a prison cell bring us courage in our own struggles to proclaim the Gospel, even in adversity. May St. John's written contributions to the Church, born of his imprisonment, continue to lead many souls to Christ. Please enliven us to follow his model of simple holiness, thus drawing ourselves and others to your mercy. Amen.

4.

Civic Holidays and Remembrances

NEW YEAR'S DAY, JANUARY 1

We gave you thanks, heavenly Father, as we begin [year]. Lead and guide us throughout the months that lie ahead. Safeguard all families, married couples, children, and other members of this community and beyond. Please inspire us to serve not only our loved ones but also our neighbors near and far. We ask this through the Lord Jesus Christ, who indeed "make[s] all things new" (Rv 21:5). Amen.

MARTIN LUTHER KING JR. DAY, THIRD MONDAY IN JANUARY

Lord Jesus Christ, may we be inspired by the faith and legacy of Rev. Dr. Martin Luther King Jr., who labored to break down walls of division between people and fought to his death for racial equality. Lead us to the unity of a collective call to holiness as we strive to make the world a better place, a more just place, a place in which we live the demands of the Gospel. Amen.

Presidents' Day, Third Monday in February

Sovereign Lord, we ask you to lay your protective hand over the people of this land. Bless and protect us, including the president as our national leader, as we strive to find opportunities to serve those both at home and abroad. We ask that you inspire us to look for ways to foster peace, harmony, and other virtuous manifestations of goodwill. We ask this in the name of Christ the Lord. Amen.

Memorial Day, Last Monday in May

Merciful Lord, as we remember those who have died in military service to our nation, stretch out your hand of mercy to their loved ones here in the United States and around the world. May they find comfort as we honor their sacrifice. Please also watch over all those who are currently serving in the United States military, and inspire them to operate with international goodwill as they defend our great land. Oh Lord, grant us peace, that we may know war no longer. We ask this in Jesus' holy name. Amen.

Independence Day, July 4

Heavenly Father, on this annual celebration of our national independence when we recognize our nation's birth on July

4, 1776, we ask that you please watch over the United States of America. Help us on our path to unity, and inspire those in positions of power to foster peace, justice, and holiness. We ask this in the name of our Lord Jesus Christ. Amen.

LABOR DAY, FIRST MONDAY IN SEPTEMBER

Dear Lord God, we give you thanks for all those who are in positions of gainful employment. Please help those who are looking for jobs, that their search may be fruitful and provide them an opportunity to provide for themselves and their families, to serve humanity, and know dignity by their work. Bless all those who labor ethically, and inspire them to remain faithful to you in all that they do. In Jesus' name, we pray. Amen.

PATRIOT DAY, SEPTEMBER 11

Lord Jesus Christ, open our hearts as we commemorate the dark day of September 11, 2001. Form in us a deeper desire for peace by the drive to work toward an end to terrorism, war, and violence of any kind. Bless our diplomats and other government officals as they continue to work for the good of all nations and all people. We ask this in your holy name as the Prince of Peace. Amen.

COLUMBUS/INDIGENOUS PEOPLES' DAY, SECOND MONDAY IN OCTOBER

Heavenly Lord, we ask that you watch over humanity on this Columbus/Indigenous Peoples' Day. As we give thanks for the gifts that have come from international exchange, we ask you for peace, harmony, reconciliation, goodwill, and respect for those with origins other than our own. Lead us to learn from the past for a better tomorrow, in which your will reigns. Amen.

VETERANS' DAY, NOVEMBER 11

Lord God, may we remain ever grateful for the men and women who have served in the armed forces of the United States. May we be inspired by their commitment to freedom and to international peace. Please encourage those who are currently serving in the military so that they may make decisions that are in line with your holy will. We ask this in the name of Jesus Christ the Lord. Amen.

THANKSGIVING DAY, FOURTH THURSDAY IN NOVEMBER

Provident God, as we celebrate Thanksgiving, may we remain grateful for the many gifts that you have given our nation and us as individuals. May our families look to you as the source of all that is good, holy, and true. May our gratitude spur us to generosity so that we share what we have with our neighbors, especially the less fortunate in our midst. In Jesus' name, we pray. Amen.

NEW YEAR'S EVE, DECEMBER 31

Lord God, we come to you grateful for the gifts that you provided to us this past year. As we gather to celebrate the changing of the year, fill our hearts with kindness and good cheer. Remain with us in the year to come so that we may use every occasion and situation to magnify your will in the interest of your kingdom. We ask this in the holy and righteous name of your Son, Jesus Christ the Lord. Amen.

5.

Regularly Scheduled Parish Activities

SACRAMENTAL PREPARATION

Before a Marriage Preparation Session

Dear Lord God, during this marriage preparation session, please grant everyone here a more profound and abiding love for you. Pour yourself into our hearts, drawing all of us to live according to your holy will. Bless all couples who are currently married, as well as those who are engaged and preparing for marriage, that [they/we] may be husbands and wives imbued with love, patience, kindness, and humility. Amen.

Before a Married Couples' Retreat

Loving God, we praise and thank you for the gift of married love. Please be with us throughout this retreat, and draw each couple to invite you into the center of their life as husband and wife. Teach husbands and wives to love and respect one another better with each passing year. As we look at ways to focus on living according to the Gospel, we make this prayer in the name of Jesus the Lord. Amen.

Before the Training of the RCIA Team

Lord Jesus Christ, lead these, your servants, to minister faithfully to those who are preparing to be baptized or to enter fully into the communion of the Catholic Church. May they always take seriously their precious role as teachers and mentors in the faith and so draw others to joyously sing your praises. We ask this in Jesus' holy and divine name. Amen.

Rejoicing for Catechumens and Candidates

Dear Lord God, we approach you with great rejoicing for our catechumens preparing for Baptism and for our candidates preparing to be received into the Church or to complete initiation through Confirmation. Remain with them and bless them and their loved ones, drawing them all into a personal, sacramental, sanctifying relationship with you. Teach this parish community to continue supporting these individuals on their journey toward fuller participation in the life and mission of your holy Church. May we all have the faith, hope, and love necessary to proclaim the Risen Lord Jesus Christ, in whose name we pray. Amen.

FOR CHILDREN PREPARING FOR THE SACRAMENTS OF BAPTISM, PENANCE, EUCHARIST, AND CONFIRMATION

Lord Jesus Christ, children were very close to you throughout your public ministry, so we are aware of the special role that they play in drawing all of us to holiness. You who instituted the Seven Sacraments, please safeguard and inspire those youth who are preparing to receive a new sacrament, whether Baptism, Penance, the Eucharist, or Confirmation. We ask this in your glorious and righteous name. Amen.

FOR LEADERS BEFORE A CHILDREN'S SACRAMENTAL PREPARATION SESSION OR RETREAT

Lord God above, pour out your love on this sacramental preparation session [retreat]. May those who are attending arrive at a better understanding of your goodness and love. Help the children come to you with open minds and eager spirits. Bless our work and guide our leadership as we seek to lead the children to friendship with you and a fuller understanding of the Church to which they belong. We ask this in the name of Jesus Christ, Lord and Savior. Amen.

BEFORE A BIBLE STUDY SESSION

Dear Lord God, you revealed yourself to us through the sacred scriptures. Bless this Bible study session as we meditate on your Word. Please give us the spiritual maturity to examine the original significance of the text and apply it fruitfully to our lives today. Draw us into an ever-deeper relationship with you by way of studying your Word. We ask this through Jesus Christ the Lord. Amen.

AFTER A BIBLE STUDY SESSION

Loving God, we thank you for the opportunity to gather in your name for this Bible study session. Please allow us to internalize and reflect on what we studied and explored in order to gain a better understanding of how it relates to the totality of sacred scripture. Help us to live what we have learned, modeling our lives more and more according to your will, and so magnify your holy name. Amen.

BEFORE A FAITH FORMATION GATHERING

Heavenly Father, please be with the catechists of this parish as we strive to bring knowledge of you to those with whom we have been called to share the Gospel, whether children, adolescents, or adults. May your will always be done, and may we look for creative and faithful ways to teach with both clarity and charity. We ask this in the name of Jesus, the ultimate Teacher. Amen.

AT THE END OF A FAITH FORMATION GATHERING

Lord God above, we come to you grateful for the chance to have experienced this time together, sharing our faith and learning about our Church. Inspire in all of us a deep and abiding desire to profess the Good News of Jesus Christ, both when convenient and when inconvenient. Please continue to pour yourself into their hearts so that they can be drawn to magnify your kingdom. We ask this through the Lord Jesus Christ. Amen.

Before the Training of Children's Catechists and Teachers at the Start of the Year

Heavenly Father, inspire all catechists and teachers in our Catholic educational institutions to be fully dedicated to leading their students to holiness throughout the coming year and beyond. May they work alongside our parish parents in promoting virtue in their students so that they may live in ever-greater accord with your holy will. We ask this in Jesus' name. Amen.

Before the Training of a Youth Ministry Team

Heavenly Father, please be with all of us gathered here, both continuing and new members of this youth ministry team. Open us to the opportunity to serve you in various capacities and locations. The gospels reveal how important youth were to your Son Jesus during his earthly ministry; draw these young men and women to serve you with faith and zeal, both during their youth and throughout their entire lives. We ask this through the same Jesus Christ the Lord. Amen.

Before the Training of a Young Adult Ministry Team

Thank you, Lord God, for the opportunity to draw young adults into an increasingly more profound relationship with you. As the members of this young adult ministry team undergo their training and take part in their various activities, bring them to find numerous creative ways to recognize, honor, and love you, living according to the Gospel of Jesus Christ, in whose name we pray. Amen.

Before the Training of the Adult Faith Formation Team

Lord God, help us to be aware of the importance of the ongoing religious formation of our parishioners. May these ministers use their gifts to lead others to a more robust comprehension of and appreciation for the Catholic faith. Shine your light on those who will participate in our programming throughout the coming months; fill them with enthusiasm for learning and the deep desire to draw ever closer to you. May all who are involved in this noble endeavor strive to accomplish this goal, in the interest of your divine kingdom. Amen.

TRAINING OF LITURGICAL AND PASTORAL MINISTRIES

TRAINING OF SACRISTANS

Lord Jesus Christ, we ask that you inspire these sacristans—both veterans and new to the ministry—to serve with joy and gratitude for the communion of the Church. Draw them into an ever deeper love for your sacraments, centering their lives on the Holy Eucharist in particular. May this experience of serving as a sacristan lead them to promote and proclaim the Good News of our salvation. We ask this in your holy and glorious name. Amen.

TRAINING OF ALTAR SERVERS

Dear Lord Jesus Christ, be with these new altar servers as they prepare to serve their priests at your holy altar. Please fill them with a profound respect for the sacramental life, centered on the Holy Eucharist: your Body, Blood, Soul, and Divinity. Allow them to serve calmly, purposefully, reverently, and intently as they strive to contribute to the kingdom of God. We ask this in your holy name. Amen.

TRAINING OF USHERS AND OTHER MINISTERS OF HOSPITALITY

Lord God, please watch over, guard, and protect those who are training to be ushers and other ministers of hospitality.

Encourage them to remain humble and devoted to service, and inspire them always to act in accord with your holy will. We ask this in the name of Jesus Christ the Lord. Amen.

TRAINING OF LECTORS

Lord God, be with our lectors as they learn how best to proclaim your Word. Grant them peace and calmness so that they may speak with clarity and solemnity. May they have zeal to share the Word along with a deep love for the sacred scriptures as a significant source of inspiration. We ask this in the name of Jesus Christ, the Word Made Flesh. Amen.

TRAINING OF EXTRAORDINARY MINISTERS OF HOLY COMMUNION

Lord Jesus Christ, give these new extraordinary ministers of Holy Communion a deep love and respect for the role that they are filling in giving your Body, Blood, Soul, and Divinity to their fellow parishioners. Please grant them steady hands, peaceful hearts, and humility, as they participate in this noble ministry. We ask this in your gracious name. Amen.

TRAINING FOR THOSE WHO DECORATE AND CLEAN THE CHURCH

Heavenly Father, we thank you for all who clean and decorate our church. We ask, Lord, that you guide and bless the work of their hands, so that this holy place where we gather together in praise and worship of you is fittingly adorned. Give them cheerful hearts and creative energy to know and love this parish community throughout each week and season of the year. In Jesus' name, we pray. Amen.

For Training of Our Music Ministers

We thank you, Lord God, for the blessing of our parish musicians, choir(s), and vocalists. May our praise of you serve this community well and lift in prayer all who gather in your holy name. Be with us as we practice and fill our hearts with joy. May every note that we produce honor you, and may we sing with joy, clarity, and zeal to celebrate the wonders of your kingdom. We make this prayer through Jesus Christ the Lord. Amen. St. Cecilia, patroness of musicians, pray for us!

Training of Ministers to the Sick

Lord God, you bring comfort and strength to those who are sick whether in body, mind, or spirit. Walk with and guide these ministers to the sick to be effective instruments of your holy will, and powerful signs of your love and tender care to our fellow parishioners who suffer with poor health. May they bring your love and peace into the homes of our brothers and sisters in need and leave them strengthened in courage and hope. In Jesus' name, we pray. Amen.

Training of a Social Justice Team or Ministers to Those in Need

Lord Jesus Christ, you spent years of your life ministering to those in challenging situations; please be with those who are training to promote social justice according to your Gospel expectations. Encourage them to act with patience and to demonstrate your preferential love. In your name, we pray. Amen.

TRAINING FOR THOSE WHO COORDINATE FUNERAL LUNCHES

God, we come to you in gratitude for those who are responsible for coordinating funeral lunches. We ask that you bless the meals that they prepare, and that their work nourish both the body and the soul. Lord, we ask for your mercy, compassion, and healing love for those who mourn. May we be for them a holy reminder of you tender care. We pray as well for the souls of all the faithful departed. May they rest in peace. Amen.

REGULARLY HELD ADMINISTRATIVE MEETINGS

BEFORE A STAFF MEETING

Lord God, open our hearts and minds to make this staff meeting fruitful. Let us be patient with one another and open to the movements of the Holy Spirit so that we have the well-being of our parishioners as our ultimate goal. We ask this in the holy name of Jesus Christ. Amen.

BEFORE A MINISTRY GROUP MEETING

Heavenly Father, we thank you for the opportunity to participate in this ministerial gathering. Inspire us to use the spiritual gifts and charisms that you have given us to glorify you and draw others into the life of discipleship. Encourage us to persevere in our ministerial engagements so that we can better serve you within and beyond our parish community. We ask this through Christ the Lord. Amen.

To Begin a Parish Council Meeting

Lord, thank you for giving us the opportunity to gather in your name today. Please grant us clarity of thought, patience, open ears, and hearts open to your will. Guide our conversations to reflect your will as we work in the interest of this parish, for the building up of this parish community, and ultimately for your greater glory. We ask this in Christ's holy name. Amen.

To Begin a Finance Council Meeting

Father, we come to you today to ask that you guide the decisions of we who are responsible for advising the pastor of our parish on his fiscal responsibilities to this community. May we members of the finance council be drawn into an ever greater awareness of our capacity to use our knowledge, experience, and skill to help foster prudent choices that will ultimately benefit this church's economic and spiritual well-being. We ask this in Jesus' redemptive name. Amen.

Before a Budgetary Review or Audit

Lord God, please help us to know that all issues and concerns, including financial ones, ultimately pale in comparison to your providence and the spiritual richness that you bestow on us. As we look at this parish's budget, inspire us to allocate resources properly and to use what we have to assist parishioners to experience you truly, especially through the sacraments. We ask this in Jesus' name. Amen.

Before a Website, Bulletin, or Other Media Meeting

Heavenly Father, author of our lives, we are grateful for the gift of literacy and knowledge. Please be with those of us who prepare parish communications. Give us clarity of mind, kindness of heart, and a genuine desire to serve our fellow parishioners. May what we produce be a source not only of information but also of inspiration and spiritual insight. Lead our parish closer to you by the work we do. We pray this in the name of Jesus the Lord. Amen.

Before a Deanery Meeting

Heavenly Father, we thank you for the opportunity to gather and discuss the status and needs of the parishes in this larger Catholic community. Please watch over these local communities, and inspire both the clergy and the laity to work together for the kingdom of God by placing the Eucharist and the other sacraments at the center of our lives. In Jesus' name, we pray. Amen.

6.

Occasional Parish Events

OUTREACH PROJECTS

BEFORE GOING TO PRAY IN FRONT OF AN ABORTION FACILITY

Holy Lord of Life, we give thanks for all human life, beginning at conception. Please be with us as we pray at the abortion provider this day. May we both promote and experience peace, goodwill, and positive regard. Pour your merciful love into the hearts of those who are considering having an abortion; may they find strength and support in their struggle so that they instead choose life. Bring healing to those who have had an abortion and guide us in acts of outreach, charity, and courageous support toward them. In Jesus' name, we pray. Amen.

Before Going to Serve the Hungry

Lord Jesus Christ, we recognize that in serving others, we are ultimately serving you. Please be with us as we prepare to go and give nourishment to the less fortunate. Let us never objectify or pity these people in need, but rather may we see in them your image and likeness. May we love them as our own, which they indeed are as children of our heavenly father. In your holy name, we pray. Amen.

To Begin a Parish Service Trip

Heavenly Father, be with us as we prepare to embark on this service trip. May our final preparations be organized, productive, and without complication. Grant us safe passage, peace, and dedication to the Gospel as we labor to make your will, not ours, be done, both during this trip and beyond. We ask this through Christ the Lord. Amen.

For Adults Serving as Mentors for Parish Youth on Service Endeavors

Heavenly Father, we thank you for the opportunity and the privilege to serve as mentors for the youth of our parish as they undertake this service initiative. Help us to share the lessons of our own experience, with the understanding that wisdom is a gift of the Holy Spirit to be shared for your greater glory. Help us to exercise prudence in what we say and do to encourage our youth. We ask this in Jesus' name. Amen.

Before a Volunteer-Run Event

Heavenly Father, we thank you for the volunteers who have come forward to assist with this event. Be their strength this day. Guide them and inspire them to use their time and talents to make this event go well. May these good people magnify the kingdom of God through their witness. In Jesus' name, we pray. Amen.

Before a Parish Fundraiser

Sovereign Lord, we ask your blessing on this parish fundraiser that we are preparing to undertake. Please be with all those who are involved in this initiative in any way. May we raise the funds necessary, ultimately glorifying you through faithful stewardship. In Jesus' name, we pray. Amen.

SOCIAL OCCASIONS

Before a Weekend Sporting Event at the Parish

Lord God, we give you thanks for the opportunity to participate in this weekend athletic event. Please be with the competitors in mind, soul, and body as they compete to your greater glory. No matter the outcome of the competition, may everyone present continue to be grateful for this occasion that you have given us for fellowship in Christ's holy name, in which we pray. Amen.

Before a Parish Party

Lord God, guide and inspire our thoughts, words, and deeds so that we act prudently during this parish party. Let us make sure that you remain at the core of all that we say and do. May this time of celebration be an opportunity for fellowship and evangelization as we strive to be disciples who serve your eternal kingdom. We ask this in Jesus' name. Amen.

Before a Parish Picnic or Festival

Heavenly Father, bless us and this food as we begin our [parish picnic/festival]. May the goodness of the food and our conversation foster healthy fellowship. Be with us in all that we say and do, ensuring that our words and deeds reflect your glory and your will for the ultimate well-being of our parish, which is centered on the sacramental meal of the Eucharist. In Jesus' name, we pray. Amen.

Before a Teen Dance or Social

Dear Lord, please guide our youth participating in this [dance/social] to make prudent, wise, and chaste decisions in how they carry themselves. Bless this occasion as an opportunity for fellowship, in the interest of your greater glory and majesty. Inspire these youth to holiness and to bringing your Good News into the world in all that they think, say, and do. We ask this in Jesus' name. Amen.

PARISH PROJECTS

FOR YOUTH COMPLETING WORK AROUND THE PARISH

Lord God, we thank you for the service of these young people. Please be with them as they complete their project so that both they and their fellow parishioners can benefit from their efforts to magnify your kingdom. Grant them safety, prudence, and openness to the work of the Holy Spirit in their lives. We ask this in Jesus' name. Amen.

FOR SUCCESS OF A CAPITAL CAMPAIGN

Dear Lord, we thank you for the opportunity to organize and facilitate this capital campaign. Please draw us to remember that the funds collected are simply a resource, yet one that we hope will benefit many facets of our parish community as we seek to serve you. Encourage donors to be generous, recalling that we are all called to store up "treasures in heaven" (Mt 6:20). We make this prayer in Jesus' holy name. Amen.

DURING BUILDING RENOVATIONS

Heavenly Father, we thank you today for the physical space that is the church building within our parish community. In the midst of renovations, may this area continue to be a spiritual haven and an oasis of sanctity for those who come to spend time with the Lord. May the celebration of the sacraments, centered on the Holy Eucharist, remain the focus of our community. We ask this in Christ's name. Amen.

For the Opening of a New Parish Facility

Lord God, grant your favor upon this new parish facility, the [name of facility]. Bless all those who will use this facility, and please ensure its safety and security. May this location bring you greater glory by giving us space to participate in your work. May every space in this parish serve as an invitation to reflect on you and your abundant goodness. We ask this in Christ's name. Amen.

For the Opening of a Parish Food Pantry, Clothes Closet, or Other Direct Care Ministry

Lord Jesus Christ, the gospels are filled with examples of how to serve others, to act charitably according to your expectations for us of holiness and righteousness. Watch over this community as we open this new [parish food pantry/clothes closet/ other direct care ministry], to draw us all ever closer to your loving embrace. We ask this in your holy name. Amen.

PEOPLE COMING AND GOING

For New Parishioners

Dear Father in heaven, today we give thanks for our new parishioner/s, [name/s]. May those who are coming into our parish community find a place of fellowship, peace, and encouragement toward holiness as we form our lives around the sacraments and God's will for us. May we celebrate family life and other features of our parish, as [name/s look/s] for ministries in which to become involved. In Jesus' name, we pray. Amen.

For Parishioners Moving from the Parish

Dear Lord, we give thanks today for the gift of [name/s] within our community. As [he/she/this couple/this family] prepares to depart from us, please remain close to [him/her/them], encouraging [him/her/them] to seek you first always. Please let [his/her/their] new parish be for them a place of joyful encounter with Christ in the sacraments, especially the Eucharist. We pray in his holy name. Amen.

For a New Staff Member

Lord Jesus Christ, we know that the Church that you founded is one body made up of many parts. Today, we celebrate our new staff member, [name], whom we are looking forward to seeing flourish within our parish community. May [name] be spiritually invigorated by the sacramental life that we promote in our parish, and may [he/she] find many opportunities to make God known, loved, and served. Amen.

For Welcoming a Visiting Cleric

Dear Lord Jesus Christ, in light of your institution of the sacraments of Holy Orders and Eucharist on that first Holy Thursday, bless [name] as we welcome him into our community. May he experience warmth, hospitality, and fellowship during his time here as we celebrate and center our lives on the wondrous gift that you gave us in the Holy Eucharist. Amen.

FOR WELCOMING A GUEST SPEAKER

Dear Lord, we give you thanks for the opportunity to welcome our visitor, [guest speaker's name], in our parish today. Open our ears and hearts to the message that [he/she] would like to share with us. Please put our guest at ease and send your Holy Spirit to provide [him/her] with the right words to draw our congregation closer to the Sacred Heart of Jesus, in whose name we pray. Amen.

FOR WELCOMING VISITORS

Lord God, help us to welcome [name/s], who [is/are] visiting our parish community. Please stir us to extend to [him/her/them] our hospitality, warmth, and good cheer. May [his/her/their] stay in our area be enjoyable, fruitful, and replete with Christian charity. Whenever [he/she/they depart/s] from us, which is an eventuality and not a hope, we hope that [he/she/they] will have experienced even more joy and welcome during [his/her/their] time with us than [he/she/they] expected. We pray this in Jesus' name. Amen.

FILLING POSITIONS

PASTORAL COUNCIL OR FINANCE COUNCIL SELECTION PROCESS

Heavenly Father, as we convene to select members for our [pastoral council/finance council], please watch over our proceedings and send the Holy Spirit to inspire us to choose wisely.

Lead the members of the [pastoral council/finance council] to serve with diligence, honor, respect, and openness to dialogue about how to best serve our parish. Help us to make patience and charity a priority. We ask this in Jesus' holy name. Amen.

In Thanksgiving for Council Selection and Those Willing to Serve

Dear Father in heaven above, we give you thanks for a successful council selection process. Please draw those who have been selected to serve faithfully, according to the demands of their position and in alignment with the Gospel. Inspire them to serve with humility, patience, zeal, and a drive to evangelize. We ask this in Jesus' name. Amen.

Launching a Search for New Staff

Dear Lord, please help us to discern the best way to seek a new staff member for our community. We implore you to guide and direct our thoughts and actions in order to bring in a new staffer who will serve faithfully and in line with the Church's teachings. We make this prayer through Jesus Christ the Lord. Amen.

In Thanksgiving for a New Hire

We thank you, Lord God, for the new member of our parish staff. Please help [him/her] to serve faithfully, diligently, and with a zeal to live according to your promises. Give [him/her] the courage to seek help when necessary and to always choose the best course of action in accord with your holy will. We ask this in Jesus' name. Amen.

For the Selection of School Board Members

Dear heavenly Father, please guide those responsible for selecting school board members to do so with seriousness, charity, and hope. May the candidates have patience and goodwill as they go through this selection process. May every decision be made in the interest of the students, who should be challenged to be current disciples and future saints. We ask this in the name of Jesus the Lord. Amen.

In Thanksgiving for Those Who Serve on the School Board

We give thanks, Lord in heaven, for those who are serving on the school board. Please give them the drive to serve the kingdom of God effectively in this unique capacity. May they be blessed with zeal and challenge students to live as current disciples and future saints. We ask this in Jesus' name. Amen.

7.

Times of Crisis or Particular Need

PARISH AND COMMUNITY

FOR AN END TO GOSSIP WITHIN THE PARISH

Dear Lord God, you are a God of truth and of charity. Please draw those who have fallen into the sinful trap of gossip to remember that you designed us for charity and goodwill. Heal those harmed by gossip, and open their hearts to forgiveness. Help those who have remained silent in the face of our current tensions discern prudent next steps. Let our words be a source of inspiration to our neighbors, lifting them up and drawing them to consider the beauty of life as a faithful disciple of Jesus Christ, in whose name we pray. Amen.

CIVIL UNREST OR CONFLICT

Heavenly Father, we are in the midst of turmoil. Rain down your healing and mercy upon us as we attempt to recover some semblance of peace in the wake of the civil unrest that we are experiencing. Pour peace into the hearts of those who have been affected, and draw our community to seek reconciliation, harmony, and goodwill. We ask this in the loving name of your Son Jesus, the Prince of Peace. Amen.

FOR THE JUST RESOLUTION OF A LOCAL LABOR DISPUTE

God in heaven above, please bring about a peaceful resolution to this labor dispute that has arisen within our community. We thank you for the opportunity to work, especially when it comes to serving others according to your will. We ask this in the holy name of Jesus Christ the Lord. Amen.

IN RESPONSE TO LOCAL JOB LOSSES

Heavenly Father, be with the many families who are experiencing challenging financial situations at this time. We recognize that there is great dignity in work; please encourage those who are struggling to find employment to remain steadfast and creative in their approaches to seeking positions that will bring them fulfillment while giving you the greatest honor. We ask this through Christ the Lord. Amen.

FOR THE RETURN OF LOVED ONES TO THE CHURCH

Dear Lord God, just as the prodigal son returned to his father's loving embrace, guide the hearts of our loved ones who no longer come to church back to us. People leave for numerous reasons, many known to you alone; teach us to be patient witnesses to the faith we hold dear. Open their minds and hearts to know that the Church, founded by Christ, is where we find unity. May they be drawn to return to the practice of the faith by our examples of faith, hope, and love. Amen.

DURING FINANCIAL DISTRESS IN THE PARISH OR WIDER COMMUNITY

Loving Father in heaven, be with us in this time of financial difficulty. We know that money is an important resource that can help us to better serve you and your kingdom when it is oriented toward your will. Please draw us to be creative with our resources in order to minister to your people and serve our community as you would have us do. We ask this in the name of Jesus Christ the Lord. Amen.

FOR AN END TO POVERTY IN OUR COMMUNITY

Lord Jesus Christ, we know from the gospels that you are close to those living in material and spiritual poverty. Enrich us with a zeal for fulfilling your will and bringing about your kingdom. Please draw us to serve those who are mired in poverty of any sort for by serving them, we are ultimately serving you. Amen.

For Calm before a Church Event

Lord, our God, be with those who may be nervous now before [name event]. Please draw those concerned to remain calm in the knowledge that you are with us and ultimately in control. Grant us peace of mind, and quell the anxiety that may be creeping in. We thank you, God, for your sovereignty. We make this prayer through the Lord Jesus Christ, Prince of Peace. Amen.

For Greater Harmony within the Parish

Dear heavenly Father, please bestow greater peace, harmony, accord, and tranquility on this community. May all parishioners experience your bounteous love and mercy and each other's friendship. May forgiveness reign in all corners of this place. May we imitate the example of the Lord Jesus Christ in all that we say and do. We ask this in the name of the same Jesus our Lord. Amen.

For Peace within a Parish Community

We come to you at this time, Lord Jesus Christ, Prince of Peace, to ask you to bring peace to the members of this parish community. Where there is discord or strife, please rest your healing hand. Please draw all of us as parishioners to embrace a spiritual maturity that better allows us to open ourselves to the good work that you want to do in us. We ask this in your holy and glorious name. Amen.

For Those Who Cannot Attend Mass Due to an Emergency

Lord Jesus Christ, please open your Sacred Heart to those for whom it is impossible to attend Mass at this time due to [inclement weather/civil strife/the unavailability of a priest/ other cause]. Please draw their minds to your holy will, and keep them safe in whatever conditions they find themselves. May they know of our love, as they look forward to returning to the sacramental life once this predicament clears. We ask this in your merciful name. Amen.

For Those Who Need Help Praying

Heavenly Father, we recognize that you will never abandon us; however, we may sometimes to think you are somehow absent from or uninterested in our lives. Please assist those who find it difficult to pray, perhaps due to distraction, hardness of heart, or another obstacle. Pour yourself into their hearts to soften them and help them respond to your divine will. Amen.

For Unity, Fidelity, and Orthodoxy in the Church

Heavenly Father, inspire in us unity, fidelity, and orthodoxy. In an era of relentless confusion, apathy, and discord, please unify your Church. Lead the laity, clergy, and religious to strive for discipleship with our eyes fixed on the demands of the Cross and our hearts set on unity. May orthodoxy, morality, and truly faithful teaching reign, for the uplifting of your kingdom. Amen.

In Thanksgiving for the Eucharist

Lord Jesus Christ, we are so thankful for the gift that you have given us in the Eucharist. Please let us never take for granted, not even for a moment, the privilege that we have in commemorating your sacrifice. May we fearlessly, proudly, and charitably proclaim to others the beauty of your True Presence—Body, Blood, Soul, and Divinity. We ask this in your divine name. Amen.

For a Couple before a Wedding

Lord Jesus Christ, we come to you in gratitude for the public witness of [names of the groom and bride] as they prepare to receive the Sacrament of Holy Matrimony. Please inspire them to live lives in accord with your holy will, opting always for beauty, goodness, and truth. May their witness inspire others to be like you in all that they say and do. In your name, we pray. Amen.

VIOLENCE, DISASTER, AND DEATH

In the Aftermath of Violence

Lord Jesus Christ, Prince of Peace, we implore you to remain with our community as we struggle to cope with the violence that has taken place within it. Bring healing to those who have been victimized and peace and reconciliation to their families.

Draw us together that we may bring an end to the violence. May harmony and accord be restored to us. We ask this in your holy name. Amen.

For Protection during Storms, Fire, Flooding, and Other Natural Disasters

Heavenly Father, we ask you please to place your provident and protective hand over this community in order to safeguard us from natural disasters and accidents, whether storms, fires, floods, or other dangerous situations [feel free to name the specific incident that is impacting the community]. We ask this in the holy name of Jesus Christ the Lord. Amen.

For Healing and Recovery after Natural Disaster

Dear Lord God above, please bring healing and peace to this community that has experienced the adversity of a natural disaster [feel free to name the specific incident that has impacted the community]. Draw us together during this time of difficulty, and inspire those who are able to provide in various ways for those who are in need. We make this in Jesus' loving name. Amen.

Following the Death of a Pastor, Staff Person, or Lay Parish Leader

Dear Father in heaven, we come to you today, mourning and sorrowful for the passing of our dear friend, [name]. Please receive [him/her] into your loving embrace, and bring peace and solace to [his/her] family. May our friend's time with us and commitment to our parish remain [his/her] legacy as we remember how [he/she] drew us closer to you. We ask this through the name of Christ the Lord. Amen.

Following the Death of a Local Civic Leader

Dear heavenly Father, we ask you to receive into your eternal presence the soul of our dearly departed community leader [name of the deceased]. Please grant consolation and healing to [his/her] family and loved ones. We are thankful for [his/her] life and hope that [his/her] legacy will continue with our call to serve others. In Jesus' name, we pray. Amen.

Following the Murder of a Parishioner

We come to you, heavenly Father, with heavy hearts as we mourn the tragic death of our friend and fellow parishioner [name of the deceased]. Please receive [him/her] into your eternally loving embrace. Console [his/her] loved ones, and bring healing and reconciliation to this community. Lord, please draw society to a greater respect for all human life and thus to an end to all violence. We ask this in Jesus' merciful name. Amen.

Following the Sudden Death of a Young Person

Lord of mercy, we often don't understand why things happen as they do and to whom they do. Our hearts are heavy with sorrow because of the sudden death of [name of the deceased], our friend and fellow parishioner. Please welcome [him/her] into heaven with you, and draw [his/her] family and loved ones to experience the peace and healing that you alone can provide. In Jesus' name, we pray. Amen.

FOLLOWING A DEATH BY SUICIDE

Merciful Father, we come to you with heavy hearts to implore that you have mercy upon the soul of [name of the deceased] and welcome [him/her] into your loving embrace. Draw us together to share comfort and strength. Shower your grace upon all who struggle with despair, depression, anxiety, and other mental illness. May they find courage to seek help when they need it, and may we find courage to reach out to them in compassion and understanding. Comfort us in our sorrow, Lord, and lead us with your light. Amen.

PERSONAL AND FAMILY

FOR PRUDENT FINANCIAL STEWARDSHIP

Lord God of providence, guide us to make prudent decisions with the resources that we have been given. Teach us to be good stewards of our money. Both in our households and within our parish, please help us, your faithful people, to use what we have to most effectively serve your kingdom. We ask this in Jesus' name. Amen.

For Couples in Struggling Marriages

Father of mercy, we come to you with sorrow and hope as we implore you to enter the hearts of married couples during times of difficulty. Please be a constant guide and source of strength and comfort. Help us, their parish family, to support them in whatever ways we are able and to keep them always in our prayers. May all your holy people act in accord with your will in these times of struggle. Through the intercession of the Holy Family and all saints who were married, we pray. Amen.

For an End to Pessimism and a Renewal of Hope

Heavenly Father, we know that anything can happen, whether for the good or for the bad, on any given day. Although we may be tempted to think negatively, or even to despair, we must recall that you are God, and it is in you that we confide, place our trust, and renew our hope. Please encourage us to be more grateful and positive, today and every day. We ask this in the hope of Christ's enduring presence here among us. Amen.

For Unity within Our Households

Lord Jesus, watch over our parish households—nuclear families, multigenerational family homes, communities of college and other young adult roommates and housemates, [the sisters' convent,] and the parish rectory. Please inspire our households to profess your goodness and your truth and to encounter unity in doing so, thus carrying out your desire for communal solidarity. Let us in this way better live according to your Gospel and so magnify your kingdom. Amen.

For Ongoing Personal Conversion

Lord Jesus Christ, you came to live among all types of sinners. You forgave then and continue to forgive now, yet always with the expectation that we leave behind our old ways. Please give us the courage and prudence to look deep within and see how we can change more to fulfill your will for us to live morally righteous lives that give both ourselves and our fellow disciples a better prospect for eternal life. Amen.

For Parental Guidance

Heavenly Father, you set the father and the mother over their children to protect, nurture, educate, and spiritually enrich them. Please inspire all parents to take this role seriously so that, following the example of the Holy Family, [they/we] may better fulfill the plans of your kingdom. We ask this of you with the understanding that you are our ultimate, sovereign parent, and we join Christ in calling you *Abba*. Amen.

For Parents of a Child Entering Adolescence

Lord God in heaven above, please watch over our child, [child's name], as [he/she] enters into adolescence. These teenage years can be challenging and filled with distractions, temptations, and societal messages that lead young people astray. May our child's guardian angel watch over [him/her], interceding for [him/her] that [he/she] stay on the right path. We ask this in Christ's name. Amen.

FOR THOSE MOVING INTO DORMS

Heavenly Father, we ask you to be with those students who are moving into the dorms at their respective colleges. Please guide them to make their living quarters into spaces of prayer, with opportunities for quiet reflection and study. May their dorms likewise serve as spaces for reasonable amounts of fellowship and goodwill. We ask this in Christ's holy name. Amen.

FOR PARENTS TRANSITIONING THEIR CHILDREN TO COLLEGE

Lord God above, grant courage to parents whose children are making the transition into college life. Responding to the intercession of these children's guardian angels, guide them to make wise, prudent, and chaste decisions throughout the coming years. Please encourage them to remain close to the sacraments, especially the Holy Eucharist and Reconciliation, and to follow you in all that they do. We ask this in Christ's holy name. Amen.

FOR PARENTS WELCOMING CHILDREN HOME ON BREAK FROM COLLEGE

Dear Lord God, please bring our college students home safely during this break. Lead us to provide a setting for peaceful and formative dialogue, drawing us all to have ever more meaningful family interactions so that we can make special memories of fellowship in your name. We ask this in the name of Jesus Christ the Lord. Amen.

For Students before Exams

Lord Jesus Christ, please help students preparing for exams to be calm and composed. Give them clarity of mind and the peace that you alone can give. Teach them to prepare well and grant them patience in this time of stress and increased anxiety. Give them the strength not only to show what they know but also to employ that knowledge for the advancement of the kingdom of God for the remainder of their lives. We ask this in your holy name. Amen.

In Thanksgiving for the End of Exams and of the Semester

Lord Jesus Christ, we thank you for the completion of exams and another semester. May our students return to their homes peaceful, strengthened, and wiser for the sake of your kingdom. Remind them that moving back to a family home can bring tensions and impatience. Ease this transition and fill our students with patience, good cheer, and compassion for their family members and other loved ones who eagerly await their return. We ask this in his holy name. Amen.

For Parishioners with Depression, Anxiety, or Other Mental Health Concerns

Merciful God, pour out your tenderness on our parishioners who live with diseases and disorders of the mind. Strengthen their courage and desire to seek assistance when they need it. Help us to faithfully accompany them, to bring them and their loved ones comfort, hope, and material assistance when we are able. Most of all, teach us as your Church not to look the other way, but to see the needs of those who struggle with mental health and be Christ for them in our loving-kindness. Amen.

For Those with Autism Spectrum Disorder and Other Behavioral Disorders

Lord God, we ask you to watch over, guide, and protect all those who have special behavioral and cognitive needs. May they know that they are loved and welcomed here at [name of parish]. Please teach us to embrace them with kindness and learn to adjust our behavior to accommodate their distinctive needs. Help these individuals and their families to recognize their gifts, and help us to value and celebrate their contributions to this community. We ask this in Jesus' name. Amen.

For Greater Humility

Lord God, we come to you today to ask that you instill in us greater humility in all that we say, do, think, and profess. Please empty us of conceit and self-centeredness so that we can better share the Gospel of your Son Jesus Christ for the building up of your kingdom. We implore you, Lord God, to draw us into a deeper understanding of the spiritual strength found in humility, which can fortify our relationships with you and with one another. Amen.

For Greater Patience

Dear Lord God, please help all of us who are struggling to practice patience. Lead us to recognize that patience is not only necessary for the well-being of this community, but also vital in the life of the disciple who aspires to heaven, since it better opens us to love both you and our neighbor. Please draw us to a more patient spirit. We ask this through Christ the Lord. Amen.

For Greater Trust and Forgiveness

We ask you, Lord Jesus Christ, to instill greater trust in us. Many of have been wounded, neglected, forgotten, or otherwise hurt, and we may find it difficult to trust. At the same time, we may have hurt others with our words, actions, or neglect. Please help us both to forgive and to be forgiven, according to your gracious will. Lord, in whom we confidently place all of our trust, we ask this in your holy name. Amen.

For Hope in the Midst of Despair

Lord God of all hopefulness, we come to you today to implore you to grant us the hope that originates in you alone. Cast despair from our lives, and allow us to rest in your provident presence. Please draw us to the spiritual security offered by the Good News of Jesus Christ, in whose name we pray. Amen.

For Parishioners Battling Addiction

Dear Lord, we ask you to place your healing hand on all in this parish who struggle with addiction. Please help them to know that they are more than this affliction. We know that you are capable of filling our hearts with hope, courage, and ultimately true peace. Bless our friends so that they too come to know your faithfulness and love. We ask this through Christ the Lord, our greatest healer. Amen.

FOR PARISHIONERS BATTLING ALCOHOLISM

Lord Jesus Christ, please draw everyone who is addicted to alcohol to your Sacred Heart. Be with these individuals and their families so that they can know that you have their best interest at heart. May those who are dealing with alcoholism regard you as the source of their inspiration and strength as they seek to remain sober. We ask this in your holy and righteous name. Amen.

FOR THOSE SUFFERING FROM ISOLATION

Lord God, we ask you to draw into your holy presence all those who are dealing with isolation, abandonment, or other types of loneliness. Please open their hearts so that they may know that they are loved deeply by you and grant them the courage to seek parish here within your Church. May we pay attention to those among us who may be alone and hurting and reach out to them in kindness. Encourage those who feel isolated to seek your will and to find comfort and strength in the Gospel of Jesus Christ. We make this prayer in his same holy name. Amen.

FOR PARISHIONERS LIVING WITH CHRONIC ILLNESS

Dear Lord God, we come to you today to ask that you place your loving and merciful hand upon our fellow parishioners who are experiencing chronic illness. Please bring them healing, peace, and an awareness of your love. We ask this in Jesus' wonderful name. Amen.

FOR MEMBERS OF THE COMMUNITY WHO ARE SICK

Lord God, please place your healing hand upon the members of this community who are dealing with serious illness. We ask you to bring them comfort, rest, and healing so that they may continue to glorify your kingdom. We ask this in Jesus' holy and righteous name. Amen.

FOR A PARISHIONER WITH A DIFFICULT PREGNANCY

We ask you, loving Father, to place your merciful and mighty hand upon all those who are experiencing difficulty with their pregnancies, especially [name]. Please grant comfort, hope, and peace to her heart and the hearts of all who are worried, and please guide the minds and hands of the medical personnel involved to help both the mother and her unborn child. We ask this in the name of Jesus, the Divine Physician. Amen.

FOR THOSE EXPERIENCING INFERTILITY

Loving God, we come to you today to ask you to be with all those who are experiencing infertility. Sometimes we do not understand your ways. Please shower your compassion on the hearts of these couples, and guide them to trust you and to know that you walk with them. Help them to find treatments that are in line with Catholic principles. Give them patience, comfort, and hope. May we all come to know ever more deeply that children are ultimately your own, a supreme gift. In Jesus' name, we pray. Amen.

FOR THOSE HOPING TO ADOPT

Father God, we thank you for your sovereignty in our lives, for the gift of all human life, and for drawing us to the embrace of your merciful and loving heart. If it is your will, please grant [couple's names] the opportunity and privilege to adopt a child and raise him or her to love and adore you. Let us continue to praise and honor you for your goodness and truth. In Jesus' name, we pray. Amen.

FOR A PARISHIONER WITH A SPECIAL INTENTION

Dear Lord, you know the inner workings of our hearts. Please be with our friend [parishioner's name] as [he/she] deals with the situation for which [he/she] has requested our prayers. Grant peace in [his/her] heart and in any set of circumstances that may arise, that all may unfold according to your divine will. We make this prayer through Jesus Christ. Amen.

FOR A PARISHIONER WHO HAS EXPERIENCED TRAUMA

Almighty Lord, it is in your sovereignty that we find solace and protection. Please draw [name] into the comfort of your presence at this time, as [he/she] has experience trauma. Allow [him/her] to remain open to your consolation and experience abiding peace, tranquility, and stability once more. In Jesus' name, we pray. Amen.

FOR AN OUTPOURING OF JOY

Lord God in heaven above, we ask you to pour out your joy upon this community, both on individuals and on the group. We understand that all joy has you as its origin; please open our hearts to the reality that you want to see us joyful and that the only path to that joy is according our lives to your holy will, per the Gospel expectations of Jesus Christ. We ask this through the same Lord Jesus, font of our joy. Amen.

FOR FAMILY AND LOVED ONES BEFORE THE START OF A FUNERAL

We give you thanks, heavenly Father, for the life of our dearly departed family member [name of the deceased]. Please receive [him/her] into paradise, and give us the strength to go on in [his/her] absence, yet always remembering the wonderful ways in which [his/her] life enriched our own. We ask this in Jesus' holy name. Amen.

IN THANKSGIVING FOR PETS

Lord God, Creator of all life, we come to you in joy and gratitude for all your glorious creation. We thank you particularly today for our pets. Since animals have so much to teach us about the wonders of nature, please draw our minds and hearts to ponder the eternal truths that you reveal through them. May we always remember the comfort and joy our pets bring to us. Help us to care for them and for all creation in ways befitting your glory. In praise of all creation, we say, "Amen!"

SOCIETAL ILLS

For an End to Abortion

Gracious Lord, you are indeed our Lord of Life. Please draw both this community and broader society to see unborn human life as a beautiful reflection of your sacred and divine self. May both legislation and the inner workings of the human heart echo the value that you have assigned to every single human life, from the moment of conception until the moment of natural death. We ask this in Christ's holy name. Amen.

For an End to Euthanasia and Physician-Assisted Suicide

Loving Lord, you are the Author of Life and therefore the origin of all that is good and holy. Teach us to spread a greater respect for all human life, including the lives of the infirm, the elderly, and others who are not afforded their proper worth. Please bring an end to euthanasia and physician-assisted suicide by inspiring both citizens and legislators to value all human life. We ask this in Christ's name. Amen.

For an End to the Persecution of the Global Church

Heavenly Father, please watch over your global Church. Be with those Christians who are suffering around the world simply because they live in witness to your divine love. Inspire your faithful disciples to exercise fortitude, prudence, and patience in carrying out their daily apostolates, all to your greater glory. We make this prayer in Jesus' holy and righteous name. Amen.

For an End to Pornography

Lord God, you fashioned humanity to reflect your goodness, holiness, and truth. Help our society cast away pornography and instead flourish with profound respect for the human body and the promotion of chastity. Please help those who are addicted to pornography to find practical spiritual guidance and courage in the Sacrament of Reconciliation. We ask this in the name of Jesus Christ the Lord. Amen.

For an End to Racism

Heavenly Father, we recognize on a daily basis that you made us as reflections of you. Please inspire throughout humanity—both inside and outside of the Church—a greater appreciation of the rich variety of ethnicities as reflections of your goodness regardless of geographic, cultural, or national background. Teach us to remove the walls of division and to respect everyone's contributions to our global community. Amen.

For an End to Sexism

Dear Lord God in heaven above, you have told us that we are all made in your image and likeness. Lead us always to regard others with respect, especially in our interactions with people of the opposite sex. Help us recall your beautiful design for humanity: that we should live in harmony as men and women. Please draw the two sexes to honor and serve rather than to objectify each other. We ask this in Jesus' holy name. Amen.

For an End to Classism

Lord God above, we are all members and participants in humanity, and we desire to make society more reflective of our common bonds. Remembering the poverty in which your Son lived and your preferential love for the poor, may we avoid judging another's worth based upon his or her wealth, material belongings, and/or social status. Please bring us to a greater humility. We ask this in Jesus' righteous name. Amen.

For an End to Discrimination against and Neglect of the Elderly

Heavenly Father, please draw us to recognize that respecting our elders reflects your love for all people. Rather than looking at older community members as some sort of impediment or inconvenience, let us view them according to the wisdom and experience that they have accrued during their long lives. May we constantly strive to learn from them, assist them when they need us, and always show patience and kindness toward them. We ask this in Jesus' holy name. Amen.

For an End to Child Abuse and Neglect

Lord God, break open the hearts of those who would abuse childern, your precious loved ones. May temporal justice be brought to abusers, and bring the fullness of healing and reconciliation to victims of abuse and/or neglect. We ask this in your healing name. Amen.

For an End to Sex Trafficking

Merciful God, we praise you for the gifts of compassion and courage. Fill our hearts with both as we face the harsh realities of sex trafficking, which remains a vicious yet largely hidden plague on our world. Teach us not to turn away from this horror, but to help end this evil and to advocate for protection of its victims. We pray in the name of Jesus, our Lord and King. Amen.

For an End to Drug Trafficking

Tender Lord, fill our hearts and minds with a sincere desire to fight the destructive forces of the illegal drug trafficking that plagues our nation and our world. May we find the courage to protect those most vulnerable to addiction and advocate for just laws and effective enforcement that can help bring an end to drug abuse. Protect first responders who face potential violence each day as they strive to make our community safer for all. We ask these things in the name of Jesus, our Lord and Savior. Amen.

For an End to Arms Trafficking

Lord God of all the earth, we pray for peace throughout the world. May we be bold in our pursuit of justice for those who are killed or otherwise severely harmed by the buying and selling of arms. May we fight for an end to violence and the greed that fuels the illegal selling of weapons across the globe. Grant us peace, O Lord. Amen.

For Increased Environmental Stewardship

Lord God, Creator of the universe. Please inspire us to protect the earth, the home you've given to us. Lead us to recall that human life is the pinnacle of all that you have made. May the natural world inspire us to greater protection of this our temporal home, for the sake of the most vulnerable within the human family and all the magnificence of your creation. May our love and care for the earth and all the life it bears teach us to strive faithfully toward our eternal home with you in heaven. We pray this in union with the Church throughout the world. Amen.

In a Time of International Crises

Dear Lord of all creation, we sometimes feel so helpless when we consider all of the strife and misery in certain parts of the world. Please place your merciful hand upon all those around the globe who are suffering dreadfully. Stir us to action against injustices so that we can serve our fellow members of the human family in a way that draws both us and them to consider the beauty of the Gospel and the prospect of eternal life in Christ. We ask this in his name. Amen.

AT A TIME OF NATIONAL EMERGENCY

We implore you, Lord, to watch over our nation as we reel from [name emergency] that has besieged it. In the midst of this dilemma, may we be encouraged to come together and seek ways of serving one another, recognizing in our common humanity our shared dignity based on your having formed us in your image and likeness. Please protect us from further peril. We ask this in the name of Jesus Christ the Lord. Amen.

FOR RESPONSIBLE INTERNET AND SOCIAL MEDIA USE

Heavenly Father, the internet and social media are opportunities to enrich our spiritual lives and to evangelize with unique approaches. However, too often they are misused, if not abused, in violation of your will. Please encourage everyone who accesses the web to do so with prudence, temperance, and fortitude. May we ensure that all of our actions reflect Christian principles. Amen.

FOR THOSE FACING SEEMINGLY INSURMOUNTABLE BUSYNESS

Heavenly Father, at any given time, we have many duties and responsibilities to fulfill. Please draw our hearts to rest in you rather than giving in to worry. Help us to organize ourselves and to assist others, since it is in helping others that we are building up the Body of Christ. We ask this through the same Christ the Lord. Amen.

FOR THOSE STRUGGLING TO LIVE CHASTELY

Lord Jesus Christ, during your public ministry, you called many who were living unchastely to leave behind their ways of iniquity and come to you as new people. We ask you, please inspire everyone from youth to married couples and those in authority positions to avoid sexual temptation and live out your plan for chastity and sexual purity. In your purest name, we pray. Amen.

8.

For Increased Virtue, Obedience, Mercy, and Holiness

THE CARDINAL VIRTUES

FOR AN INCREASE IN THE CARDINAL VIRTUES

We ask you, most virtuous Lord Jesus Christ, to encourage us as we attempt to live according to the cardinal virtues of fortitude, justice, prudence, and temperance. It is our hope that through living the cardinal virtues we will become better equipped to embrace the overarching theological virtues of faith, hope, and love and imitate your holy will in all that we do. In your righteous name, we pray. Amen.

For an Increase in Fortitude/Courage

Heavenly Father, please give us a profound desire to increase our fortitude in sharing the faith. May we have more courage in living the life of the faithful disciple, constantly endeavoring to embrace and practice holiness, even when it is difficult or inconvenient. We ask this in the holy name of Jesus Christ the Lord. Amen.

For an Increase in Justice

Dear Lord God, draw your faithful to labor for a more just and rightly ordered society. Inspire us to work against injustices where they occur so that we can show greater love to our fellow members of the human family. Let us respect the inherent and God-given dignity of all human life, from the moment of conception until the moment of natural death. May we strive for greater justice in furthering the kingdom of God, from whom all order flows. In Jesus' name, we pray. Amen.

For an Increase in Prudence/Wisdom

Heavenly Father, please pour yourself into our hearts so that we can better put into practice the virtue of prudence. Help us find models of this virtue in our community and to avoid improper thoughts and harmful behaviors. Help us to steadily acquire wisdom throughout our lives, comprehending that prudence ultimately directs us to the wisest choice possible: that of following your will. In Jesus' name, we pray. Amen.

FOR AN INCREASE IN TEMPERANCE/MODERATION

Lord God, please help us to practice the virtue of temperance. Excess, indulgence, pleasure, decadence, and other idols with false promises, make it easy to become distracted from what ultimately matters. Teach us to moderate our behavior and to pursue holiness as both an ideal and a possibility. Draw us to imitate the virtue and piety of the Lord Jesus Christ, in whose name we make this prayer. Amen.

THE THEOLOGICAL VIRTUES

FOR AN INCREASE IN THE THEOLOGICAL VIRTUES

Heavenly Father, please grant us a better appreciation for the opportunity to practice the three theological virtues of faith, hope, and love. May faith, hope, and love, all of which have their origin in you, abound in our lives and therefore build up your kingdom by reflecting the promises of the Gospel. We ask this in the name of Jesus Christ the Lord. Amen.

FOR AN INCREASE IN FAITH

Dear Lord, we come to you today because it can often be a challenge to embrace and maintain our faith as various worldly worries creep in and weaken our belief. Please fortify our faith, thereby allowing us to share the Gospel with others and strengthen their faith in the process. We ask this in Jesus' holy and glorious name. Amen.

For an Increase in Hope

Heavenly Father, source of all goodness, truth, and hope, we come to you to ask you to strengthen our hope. Please lead us to a greater understanding of the beautiful promises that you have given to us so that we can know the many reasons that we have to look forward to their fulfillment. We ask this while hoping in the Gospel per the affirmations of Jesus Christ, in whom we now pray. Amen.

For an Increase in Love

Dear God, we know from the sacred scriptures that you are love itself. Pour yourself into our hearts so that we may better manifest our love to you and to our neighbors. Please help us to fathom what is meant by Christian love, including its demands and expectations. We ask this in the name of Jesus Christ the Lord. Amen.

THE TEN COMMANDMENTS

For Inspiration to Follow the Ten Commandments

Heavenly Father, we thank you for your Ten Commandments. Far beyond mere rules to follow or burdens to carry, they are boundaries within which we can better know, love, and serve you. Please help us to live according to your holy will, for our own spiritual well-being and that of our neighbor. We ask this in the righteous name of him who followed your will perfectly: your Son Jesus Christ the Lord. Amen.

THE FIRST COMMANDMENT

"I am the Lord, your God; you shall not have strange gods before me." Lord God, please help us to remove the false idols from our lives. Help us to focus on you as the one true God, who alone are sovereignly capable of sanctifying, saving, and redeeming us. We thank you for who you are, dear Lord, and ask you to watch over us always. In Jesus' name, we pray. Amen.

THE SECOND COMMANDMENT

"You shall not take the name of the Lord, your God, in vain." Dear Lord, lead us to recall the power of words. You designed us in your image and likeness and therefore desire for us to offer to the world only that which is holy, whether in word or deed. Please draw us never to take you for granted and to use words that honor you and are fitting for worship. We ask this in Jesus' name. Amen.

THE THIRD COMMANDMENT

"Remember to keep holy the Lord's Day." Dear Lord Jesus Christ, every Sunday—the first day of the week—we remember your Resurrection on that first Easter Sunday. Please lead us to view every Sunday as a small Easter and to attend Mass not merely as an obligation, but as an opportunity to worship you and thus begin our week with you in the foreground. We ask this in your holy name. Amen.

THE FOURTH COMMANDMENT

"Honor your father and your mother." God the Father, God the Son, and God the Holy Spirit, it was over the family that you placed a husband and a wife, a father and a mother, to guide your children. We are inspired by the example of the Holy Family of Jesus, Mary, and Joseph; please draw society to an ever-deeper understanding of the divine orientation of the fatherly and motherly roles that you have provided. Please protect all children, and give parents patience so that they can lovingly build up their children in a warm, joyful domestic church. In Jesus' name, we pray. Amen.

THE FIFTH COMMANDMENT

"You shall not kill." Lord God, we live in an era in which human life is increasingly disregarded and unprotected. Watch over and safeguard all human life, from the moment of conception until the moment of natural death. Please inspire us to work toward an end to abortion, capital punishment, gang violence, weaponized violence in the streets, war, terrorism, euthanasia, physician-assisted suicide, other kinds of suicide, and all other denials of the sanctity of human life. We ask this in the name of Jesus Christ, the Lord of Life. Amen.

THE SIXTH COMMANDMENT

"You shall not commit adultery." Dear heavenly Father, we ask you to watch over all married couples. May husbands and wives better commit themselves to their marital vows for the well-being of their own souls, for the well-being of any children, and for all society. Please inspire the faithful to work toward an end to pornography, unchaste media, and other manifestations of sexual immorality. We ask this through the intercession of the Holy Family of Jesus, Mary, and Joseph. Amen.

THE SEVENTH COMMANDMENT

"You shall not steal." Dear Lord God, help us to work toward a society in which others' possessions—material, intellectual, or otherwise—are protected. Guide us to be more effective stewards of our time, talent, and treasure. Please lead us to work to reduce materialism, consumerism, and idolatry per the First, Ninth, and Tenth Commandments. We ask this in Jesus' holy name. Amen.

THE EIGHTH COMMANDMENT

"You shall not bear false witness against your neighbor." Almighty Father, we implore you to draw society to a greater degree of honesty. So many falsehoods, deceptions, and outright lies are being promulgated in our day. Please lead your faithful to speak only the truth, with both clarity and charity. We ask this in the name of him who is Truth itself, the Lord Jesus Christ. Amen.

The Ninth Commandment

"You shall not covet your neighbor's wife." Dear Father in heaven, please draw us to a more chaste and modest society, working against the sins of lust and covetousness. Please lead us to follow your holy will in our lives so that we can better serve your eternal kingdom by imparting the timeless Good News of the Lord Jesus Christ, in whose name we pray. Amen.

The Tenth Commandment

"You shall not covet your neighbor's goods." Lord God of heaven and earth, please help us to banish all envy and covetous desires from our lives. Draw us to a greater appreciation for what we have and for living modestly, thereby fending off materialism, consumerism, idolatry, and other mindsets that draw us away from your love as our sovereign Lord. We ask this in the name of Jesus Christ the Lord. Amen.

THE CORPORAL WORKS OF MERCY

For Inspiration to Perform the Corporal Works of Mercy

Dear Lord, inspire us to put our faith into action. Please lead us to perform the corporal works of mercy with zeal, love, humility, and joy reinforced by a prayer life centered on the sacraments. Draw us to be the face of Christ to so many who are in need, both in our communities and throughout the world. We make this prayer in the name of Jesus Christ the Lord. Amen.

BURY THE DEAD

Heavenly Father, we ask you to instill in us an abiding respect for those who have died. Have mercy on their souls, grant them eternal rest, and welcome them into the light of eternal life. Fill us with a spirit of generosity and attentiveness so that we make time to attend funeral services of those we have known in this life. Teach us to comfort those who mourn and honor their loved ones who have passed away. As we remember and honor the bodies of those who have died, draw us into a profound and lasting appreciation for the opportunity to live a life striving to follow your holy will. We ask this in Jesus' name. Amen.

FEED THE HUNGRY

Dear Lord Jesus Christ, the gospels are filled with accounts of you reaching out to those living in poverty or otherwise hungry. Inspired by your example of recognizing others' inherent human dignity and worth, may we also look for opportunities to give to those who are living in hunger or other conditions of need. We ask this in your holy name. Amen.

GIVE ALMS TO THE POOR

Merciful Lord, at the end of our earthly life, we cannot take anything with us. Please detach us from our material belongings and money, and draw us into a deeper love for neighbor.

Help us remember you have a preferential option for the poor. May we more readily place our time, talent, and treasure at their service. We ask this in Jesus' name. Amen.

GIVE DRINK TO THE THIRSTY

Heavenly Father, there are so many in our world who are thirsting, whether physically or spiritually. Please encourage us to satisfy the thirst of those around the world who are in need of access to fresh, clean drinking water. Inspire us to help satisfy spiritual thirst and bring others to the Living Water, of which the only source is your eternal Son Jesus Christ. We ask this through the same Jesus Christ the Lord. Amen.

SHELTER THE HOMELESS

Lord Jesus Christ, when your mother, Mary, and foster-father, Joseph, were preparing to welcome you into the world, so many doors were closed in their faces as they sought refuge. You were born in a humble stable. You came into the world feeling the cold sting of homelessness. Allow us to see your face as we serve those without shelter. We ask this in your holy name. Amen.

VISIT THE IMPRISONED

Merciful Father, we are often unaware of why people end up imprisoned. In many cases, it is necessary in order to protect society from danger. In other cases, however, they may have been unjustly punished. Either way, please encourage us to visit those who are detained, many of whom come to learn and follow the Gospel while incarcerated. Let us pray for all inmates, that they may come to know and experience your boundlessly merciful love. We ask this through Christ the Lord. Amen.

Visit the Sick

We thank you, heavenly Father, for the opportunity to serve those who are living in situations of physical adversity, whether infirmity, injury, physical impediment, or another circumstance. Please give us the compassion to visit with them and make your love known. Draw us to serve them according to your will, not ours. In Jesus' merciful name, we pray. Amen.

THE SPIRITUAL WORKS OF MERCY

For Inspiration to Perform the Spiritual Works of Mercy

Lord Jesus Christ, we need the inspiration to serve those whose difficulty is not necessarily physical, but spiritual. We know only you can make us whole spiritually. Help us witness your love to those suffering so that they can better know and understand what you want to do in their hearts. We make this prayer in your holy and healing name. Amen.

ADMONISH THE SINNER

Heavenly Father, one of the greatest challenges in the Christian life is identifying to a neighbor how sin is impeding his or her relationship with God. May we be sure to look inward first, resolving our own impediments. Then may we invite others, based on our love for them, to consider how they, too, can grow closer to the Lord by abandoning their sinful ways and instead pursuing virtue. Help us remember that while we can judge a person's actions, only you can judge their soul. Please give us the courage to begin and maintain those difficult conversations. May it ultimately be the Holy Spirit speaking, and not us with our own flawed egos. We pray this in Jesus' name. Amen.

BEAR WRONGS PATIENTLY

Lord God, it is often a challenge for us to bear wrongs patiently and respond in a Christian manner. Please help us to be more charitable in how we react to an infraction against us, whether perceived or real. May we act with love and mercy toward anyone who has wronged us, meanwhile offering up our suffering by attaching it to the Cross. We ask this in Jesus' righteous name. Amen.

COMFORT THE SORROWFUL

Heavenly Father, it is your will for us to bring comfort to those who are downcast. No matter what has befallen our neighbor, please draw us to offer a spiritually comforting response to his or her distress. Let us act with empathy, compassion, and attention that is the fruit of our love for neighbor per the expectations of the Gospel of Jesus Christ. We ask this in his holy name. Amen.

COUNSEL THE DOUBTFUL

Lord God above, it seems that many are leaving behind the Gospel, preferring worldly ways instead. Others are openly questioning whether you exist at all. Still others are so wounded that they cannot fathom a loving Father. Please keep us from despair and provide us with the patience to share the joy we receive from a lasting personal relationship with you, who alone can satisfy our deepest needs. Amen.

FORGIVE INJURIES

Lord Jesus Christ, forgiveness is a theme that runs through the gospels. Yet as with other virtuous acts, forgiving is easier to expect from others than to put into practice ourselves. Please draw us to have more forgiving hearts and to regard others with the same mercy that we would want to receive from them. We ask this in your lovingly merciful name. Amen.

INSTRUCT THE IGNORANT

Dear Lord God, make of us lifelong learners and guide us to be patient as we share with others what we learn and observe not only about our Catholic faith but also about our wonderful, if also sinful, world. Please lead us to draw others to consider the depths of God's love and his subsequent plan for their lives. We ask this in Jesus' virtuous name. Amen.

Pray for the Living and the Dead

Heavenly Father, we are often so busy, with so much going on at any given time. Help us remember to pray fervently throughout the day, not only for those who are still alive here with us, but also for those who have gone before us and may be experiencing a period of torment in purgatory. Please have mercy on the souls in purgatory, and grant their release into eternal repose with you. We ask this in Jesus' glorious name. Amen.

GIFTS OF THE HOLY SPIRIT

For an Outpouring of the Gifts of the Holy Spirit

Lord God, we ask you to bestow upon us the seven gifts of the Holy Spirit: counsel, fear of the Lord, fortitude, knowledge, piety, understanding, and wisdom. Please give us the courage to open ourselves to these gifts of the Holy Spirit, that we might be more capable of living faithfully according to the Gospel and drawing others to do likewise. In Jesus' name, we pray. Amen.

For Counsel

Holy Spirit, pour upon us your gift of counsel, that we might improve our ability to share with others advice that is based on Christ's promises. May our counsel be God-centered rather than self-centered. We ask this in Jesus' name. Amen.

For Fear of the Lord

Holy Spirit, pour upon us your gift of fear of the Lord, ensuring that we maintain a relationship of respect and deference to the One Triune God. May he continue to reign as our sovereign Lord. We ask this in Jesus' name. Amen.

For Fortitude

Holy Spirit, pour upon us your gift of fortitude. We need your strength to spiritually enliven us each day. We need this fortitude particularly when it comes to preferring God's holy will to our own worldly inclinations. We ask this in Jesus' name. Amen.

For Knowledge

Holy Spirit, pour upon us your gift of knowledge. Please guide us to use what we know not for selfish gain, but in order to spread the Gospel and thus make the world a better place, for the ultimate glorification of the kingdom of God. We ask this in Jesus' name. Amen.

For Piety

Holy Spirit, pour out upon us your gift of piety, that our relationship with the Triune God may be founded on our quest for personal holiness. Please draw us to seek always the Father's will and purify our hearts that we may know holiness in this life and the next. We ask this in Jesus' name. Amen.

For Understanding

Holy Spirit, pour upon us your gift of understanding, that we may better comprehend how truly deeply you love us and want what is ultimately best for us. Please guide us to trust your holy will and therefore live increasingly in accord with it. We ask this in Jesus' name. Amen.

For Wisdom

Holy Spirit, pour upon us your gift of wisdom. Please humble us so that we may fathom that you alone are omniscient, omnipotent, omnipresent, and omnibenevolent. May our wisdom draw us to align our will with yours more and more. We ask this in Jesus' name. Amen.

AGAINST THE DEADLY SINS

Against the Seven Deadly Sins (General)

Lord God, protect us from the forces of darkness in our lives. Send the Holy Spirit to help us to work against the seven deadly sins, conquering avarice, envy, gluttony, lust, pride, sloth, and wrath wherever they may manifest themselves in our lives. Please guide us instead to practice the theological virtues of faith, hope, and love, supported by the cardinal virtues of fortitude, justice, prudence, and temperance. We ask this in the holy name of Jesus the Lord. Amen.

AGAINST AVARICE

Lord God, please help us to work against avarice in our lives. Draw us to be content with what we have and to appreciate the many gifts that you reliably bestow upon us, the most important of which are spiritual gifts. We ask this in the name of Jesus the Lord, whose holiness we are called to imitate. Amen.

AGAINST ENVY

Lord God, please help us to work against envy in our lives. May we detach ourselves from an unhealthy preoccupation with what others have, especially when we are not entitled to it. Help us to be more humble. We ask this in the name of Jesus the Lord, whose holiness we are called to imitate. Amen.

AGAINST GLUTTONY

Lord God, please help us to work against gluttony in our lives. Help us to practice the cardinal virtue of temperance so that we are more moderate in what we acquire and consume. We ask this in the name of Jesus the Lord, whose holiness we are called to imitate. Amen.

AGAINST LUST

Lord God, please help us to work against lust in our lives. Help us to both practice and promote chastity, including the reservation of sexual intimacy for a husband and wife within the sacred and loving bond of marriage. Help us see abstinence and celibacy as gifts that make us more free to love you and our neighbors. We ask this in the name of Jesus the Lord, whose holiness we are called to imitate. Amen.

AGAINST PRIDE

Lord God, please help us to work against pride in our lives. Our will may be powerful, but the more we seek to appreciate your deep and abiding love for us, the more we can replace it with yours. Help us to be more humble. We ask this in the name of Jesus the Lord, whose holiness we are called to imitate. Amen.

AGAINST SLOTH

Lord God, please help us to work against sloth in our lives. We may not always feel like laboring for the kingdom of God, but we need to make the spiritual—and physical—effort if we aspire to seek your holy will for us. Help us to have greater zeal to be righteous and virtuous. We ask this in the name of Jesus the Lord, whose holiness we are called to imitate. Amen.

AGAINST WRATH

Lord God, please help us to work against wrath in our lives. Anger is an emotion that can get the better of us if we do not know how to address and control it. Please help us to find healthy ways to lay aside our anger for the well-being of our relationships and our souls. Help us to be more temperate. We ask this in the name of Jesus the Lord, whose holiness we are called to imitate. Amen.

9.

Occupations, Vocations, and Stages of Life

FOR ACCOUNTANTS AND MATHEMATICIANS

Thank you, dear Lord, for having bestowed on humanity the capacity to form reasoned thoughts and engage in logical exercises. Please guide all mathematicians, accountants, and others involved in numerical work to see you in the midst of their labors. Help us calculate how best to serve you, especially through how we serve humanity. In your perfect name, we pray. Amen.

For Businesspeople, Economists, and Financiers

We give you thanks, heavenly Father, for all those who are involved in noble pursuits within entrepreneurship, enterprise, commerce, economic and financial matters, and other business realms that are in accord with Christian principles. Please encourage them always to operate so as to embrace and advance the ideals of the Gospel. We ask this in Jesus' holy name. Amen.

For Catholic Campus Ministers and Chaplains

Thank you, Lord Jesus Christ, for inspiring all campus ministers, chaplains, and others involved in direct ministry, to follow your will in all that they do. Please draw them to find and implement unique ways to draw souls to Christ and therefore to the practice of his Good News. We ask this through the same Jesus Christ the Lord. Amen.

For Catholic Educators (Catechists, Teachers, and Professors)

Holy Lord God, we come to you today in gratitude for all those who are involved in passing along the Catholic faith. Please be with all Catholic catechists, classroom teachers, and college professors. May they steadily endeavor to instruct their students faithfully, urging them to be current disciples and future saints. We ask this in Jesus' holy and righteous name. Amen.

For Catholic Politicians

Heavenly Father, please safeguard and encourage all Catholics in political life to both advance and live according to the Good News of your Son Jesus Christ. May they never be tempted to operate according to whim, pretension, or power; rather, may they remain humbly devoted to serving the Gospel for the promotion of the common good. We ask this in the name of Jesus Christ the Lord. Amen.

For Computer Scientists

Almighty Father, please direct the minds and hearts of everyone involved in the computer industry to follow your holy will. Given the importance and remarkable influence of computers in the modern world, may these computer scientists know the critical nature of their work. May they embrace the demands of the Gospel in order to invite God's grace into their duties. Amen.

For Construction Workers and Architects

Dear Lord God, we come to you in gratitude for all those who work in architecture and building. May they be safe as they plan for and execute various projects, and may they know how appreciated they are for their contributions to fortifying the spaces that we inhabit. Please bless them and keep them secure so that they can focus on the eternal spiritual mansion that is your kingdom. In Jesus' name, we make this prayer. Amen.

For Custodial Staff

Heavenly Father, we give you thanks for all custodial staff who help our different communities to function on a day-to-day basis. Please bless them for helping to keep our surroundings clean and in good working order. May we never take them for granted, and may we always look for ways to show our appreciation to them for all that they do. In Jesus' name, we pray. Amen.

For Firefighters and EMTs

Lord God, we implore you to be with and protect all those who work in emergency medicine and rescue operations, especially firefighters, EMTs, flight nurses, and others charged with bringing the sick and injured to safety. Grant them wisdom and charitable hearts to help put their patients at ease as they seek additional medical care. Ultimately, help them to care for their patients' souls in addition to the needs of their bodies. Amen.

For Government Employees

Lord Jesus Christ, you taught us to render to Caesar and to God what is due to each. Watch over and guard those who are employed in government so that they may serve their fellow citizens well. Guide their work to ensure that it is noble, and if they encounter a task that interferes with the legitimate exercise of their faith, please give them the prudence to respond accordingly, even if it requires courage. We ask this in your holy name. Amen.

For Lawyers

Lord God, please inspire all those in the legal field, including lawyers, attorneys, judges, legislators, and policymakers, to always act in accord with your holy and divine will. Draw them to enact and further laws and outcomes that are truly in line with Gospel teaching. We ask this in the holy name of the Lord Jesus Christ, who is the Law itself. Amen.

For Medical Personnel

Holy Father, please guide the hands and minds of all medical professionals—doctors, nurses, physicians, and others charged with caring for our bodies—to take good care of their patients. Yet beyond merely handling physical concerns, may they collaborate and strive to safeguard the mental, emotional, and ultimately spiritual well-being of their patients. In the name of Jesus, the Divine Physician, we pray. Amen.

For Those Serving in the Military

Heavenly Father, watch over [name] while [he/she] undertakes military service in defense of our nation. Guard, protect, and inspire the many men and women who have placed themselves in harm's way in order to safeguard and promote freedom. Foster peace and goodwill globally, bringing an end to war, terrorism, famine, and other human rights tragedies as we strive to better the world. Amen.

For Police Officers

Heavenly Father, it is often difficult to fathom all that police officers must do every day in order to ensure the safety of their communities. Provide them with guidance, prudence, good judgment, and sincerity as they protect us. Protect them so that they can continue to serve faithfully, ultimately looking to serve you foremost. In Jesus' name, we pray. Amen.

For Psychologists and Therapists

Almighty Father, please be with psychologists and therapists as they endeavor to bring their patients to mental, emotional, and spiritual wholeness. Send the Holy Spirit to provide them with the correct words, actions, discernment, and resolution to bring healing to their patients. Be with them and their patients during dark, difficult times, instilling in them the reality of hope. Amen.

For Public Works Personnel and Tradespeople

Dear Father, we come to you with hearts grateful for all of the many men and women who are involved in public works and the various trades, including carpenters, mechanics, plumbers, electricians, and so forth. Recalling that St. Joseph and Jesus Christ himself were both in the carpentry trade, may we never stop appreciating those in the service fields for the vital work they do. May they always be inspired by the example of your Son Jesus Christ, in whose name we make this prayer. Amen.

For Restaurant, Catering, and Food Service Personnel

Heavenly Father, we give thanks for all those who are involved in planning, preparing, cooking, and serving the meals that we enjoy. Please bless their hands and pour yourself into their hearts so that they can view what they do not merely as a job, but as an opportunity to encounter the other. May their labors therefore never be taken for granted but always appreciated. We ask this in the name of the Lord Jesus, who showed us how to serve graciously. Amen.

For Retail, Commercial, and Customer Service Employees

Lord God, please watch over and protect all those employed in retail and commercial enterprises, as well as those in roles involving customer service. Shower patience on all of the parties in these settings so that both the employees and those they serve can enjoy interacting and can extend Christian love. We ask this in Jesus' righteous name. Amen.

For Scientists

Creator God, originator of the entire universe, shower down your blessings on all faithful scientists. Draw them to fathom, appreciate, and impart to others the beauties of the scientific realm so that they may grow to better proclaim the wonders of your holy name. Please watch over them and inspire them to ensure that their research is moral and centered on gospel principles. We make this prayer through Christ the Lord. Amen.

For Transportation Workers

Lord God, please bless all workers in the field of transportation: those in the automotive industry, those in aviation, drivers, truckers, boaters, train operators, and those in any position that relates to ensuring the safe, efficient transportation of people around the globe. Please encourage them to bring the Good News of Jesus Christ with them wherever they go. In the same Christ, we pray. Amen.

For Writers and Journalists

Heavenly Father, we are thankful for the gift of literacy, since it permits us to receive, share, transmit, and discuss the Gospel more easily. Please watch over and inspire all of the faithful who are involved in writing, journalism, and other media-related professions. Please provide them with the clarity of mind to impart your will to a weary world. In Christ's name, we pray. Amen.

For Those Who Are Unemployed

Lord God, please guide and help those parishioners who are now without employment. Teach us as their parish family to help ensure that their basic temporal needs are met. Grant us kindness and compassion that we may support these individuals and families in this time of uncertainty and stress. May the unemployed throughout this parish and our city soon find work that helps them to thrive. St. Joseph the Worker, pray for us! Amen.

For Those Who Are Underemployed

Heavenly Father, please help those who are currently struggling with underemployment. Give them patience and the gift of persistence. Help them to find employment that is more in line with their needs and those of their families. St. Joseph the Worker, pray for us! Amen.

For Those Discerning a Career Change

Lord God, please pour yourself into the hearts of all those who are considering changing careers. Help them to find a career that is both gainful and noble. Draw them to remember that you call us to serve you in various ways and that the Holy Spirit will help them to discern what they should do. We ask this in the holy name of Jesus the Lord. Amen.

RETIRING PARISH PERSONNEL

For a Retiring Catechist or Director of Religious Education

Heavenly Father, we give you thanks for the ministry that [name] carried out during [his/her] time here as a [catechist and/or director of religious education]. Please continue to watch over [him/her] and to inspire [him/her] to continue to draw souls to Jesus Christ through instruction in the Gospel. We ask this in Jesus' holy and glorious name. Amen.

For a Retiring Catholic Educator

We thank you, Lord Jesus Christ, for the time that [name] spent in our community. Bless [him/her] for [his/her] labors in the vineyard. Please grant [him/her] a restful retirement that offers opportunities for [him/her] to continue to teach others about the Good News of Jesus Christ. We ask this in the name of the same Jesus Christ the Lord. Amen.

For a Retiring Choir Director or Music Minister

We thank you, heavenly Father, for the music that filled this community through the leadership of [name]. As [he/she] prepares to retire, please grant [him/her] the opportunity to rest in you as [he/she] meditates on the harmonious congruity of the Gospel. Bless [him/her] and draw [him/her] to continue to bring music into a world in need of the spiritual symphony of Christ's selfless love. We ask this through his virtuous name. Amen.

For a Retiring Deacon

We thank you, Lord God above, for the various ministerial initiatives that your servant Rev. Mr. [name] undertook. Please provide him with the inspiration to continue serving your Church in some capacity as he prepares both his soul and others' for the possibility of an eternity with you in paradise. We ask this in the name of Jesus the Lord. Amen.

For a Retiring Groundskeeper/Landscaper

We come to you, dear heavenly Father, to thank you for the many ways in which [name] has beautified and fortified the grounds of this parish community. We offer our gratitude for [his/her] contributions, and ask that you bless [name] at this time. Please draw us to remain appreciative of the many people who help this parish to operate throughout the liturgical year, always centered on the Eucharist and the sacramental life. We make this prayer in the name of Jesus the Lord. Amen.

For a Retiring Parish Housekeeper or Cook

Lord God, we thank you for the many ways in which our beloved parish [housekeeper/cook], [name], built up our community through [his/her] service. We give you thanks for [his/her] example of humility and perseverance. Please be with [him/her] in retirement so that [he/she] may rest in your Sacred Heart. We make this prayer in the name of the most holy and merciful Jesus Christ the Lord. Amen.

For a Retiring Parish Priest

Lord Jesus Christ, we come to you in gratitude today for the priestly ministry that your servant Fr./Msgr. [name] undertook. As we express to you our gratitude for his ministerial service, we ask you please to remain with him in retirement as he continues to focus on the consecration of the Eucharist and the other sacraments. We ask this in the name of the Priest of Priests, the Lord Jesus Christ. Amen.

For a Retiring Religious Brother

As he enters into retirement, we thank you, Lord God, for the brotherly example offered by your servant Br. [name]. Please be with him and guide him to seek opportunities to serve you and profess the Good News of the Lord Jesus Christ. May Br. [name] continue to be enthused by the Gospel and the sacramental life, thereby steadily drawing souls heavenward. We make this prayer in the name of Jesus the Lord. Amen.

For a Retiring Religious Priest

We give thanks to you, heavenly Father, for the rich priestly ministry of Fr. [name]. As he prepares to enter into retirement, we ask that you please remain deep within his heart, continuing to enliven him to center himself on the Eucharist and your Gospel. May his life be increasingly enriched by the Good News of Jesus Christ, in whose name we make this prayer. Amen.

For a Retiring Religious Sister

Loving Father, we extend to you our sincere gratitude for the Christian duties that Sr./Mother [name] performed during her time in active ministry. Please be with her, dear Father, in her retirement so that she can continue to encounter new opportunities to serve you and thereby share the Gospel. Please help her thus to embrace and further the Good News of your Son Jesus Christ, in whose name we now pray. Amen.

VOCATIONAL DISCERNMENT

For Those Discerning God's Call/Their Vocation

Lord God, please stir the hearts of those who are open to what you are calling them to do. Clarify for them the vocation that you would like them to live. As they discern and hopefully accept their vocation, provide them with an abundance of grace to complete your holy will in their lives. We ask this through the name of Jesus the Lord. Amen.

For Those Discerning a Vocation to Marriage

Heavenly Father, we celebrate with joy that marriage was the first sacrament that appeared in the scriptures. Please watch over all those who are called to marriage so that they may know that you will reinforce what you have called them to by your holy will. May the Holy Family watch over husbands, wives, and any children that you may give them, every single one of which is a gift. Amen.

For Those Discerning a Vocation to the Priesthood

Lord Jesus Christ, you who instituted the Sacrament of Holy Orders on that first Holy Thursday, open the hearts of young men to discern a call to the priesthood. Please draw those whom you are calling to consider what a spiritual privilege it is to bring the sacraments to others within the Church. Please lead them to respond to your call with courage, zeal, and charity. We ask this in your holy name. Amen.

FOR THOSE DISCERNING A VOCATION TO RELIGIOUS LIFE

Lord God, safeguard the hearts of those whom you are calling to religious life so that they can respond courageously and faithfully with a "yes" that echoes and reflects their aptitude to devote their lives to furthering the Gospel in the interest of your kingdom. Please provide them with the support needed to enter into the community to which they are called, and may your call be confirmed. In Jesus' name, we pray. Amen.

FOR THOSE DISCERNING A VOCATION TO THE CELIBATE SINGLE LIFE

Heavenly Lord, help us see the celibate single life as a gift that allows us to love you and our neighbors more freely. Please draw those whom you have called to the celibate single life to peace in following your will, that they may understand their vocation as a means of providing a faithful witness of discipleship. Amen.

STAGES OF LIFE

FOR AN ENGAGED COUPLE

Heavenly Father, we ask you to bless, safeguard, and protect this engaged couple. May [names] together enjoy this time of preparation for marriage. Free them from undue worries about their upcoming wedding and help them find joy in uniting their families. Please give them the wisdom and courage they may need to live chastely. Help all couples—both currently and eventually engaged—to understand the demands and rewards of married life as they learn more about it. In Jesus' name, we pray. Amen.

FOR MARRIED COUPLES

We give you praise, Father in heaven, for having placed husband and wife at each other's side in order to show your face to all whom they meet. Joined in love, may the married couples of this parish serve one another, their families, and our broader community. Please bless all married couples so that their love will foster romance and genuine passion for the life they share. May every husband and wife support the other physically, emotionally, mentally, and spiritually so that they can more effectively work toward heaven. In Jesus' holy name, we pray. Amen.

FOR THE DOMESTIC CHURCH

Dear Lord God, you placed the husband and wife within the family structure to protect and nurture their children together.

Please bless and fortify every family to better reflect the fullness of love that stems from the Triune God of Father, Son, and Holy Spirit. Guide and encourage every married couple to work toward one another's holiness, as well as that of their children. We ask this in Christ's holy name. Amen.

For Mothers

Mary, Our Lady, please intercede for all of your fellow mothers today. Ask your Son, our beloved brother, the Lord Jesus Christ, to watch over and bless the mothers of our parish. May they know their true and irreplaceable worth so that they can better magnify the Lord in light of his eternal promises. We ask this in the name of your Son Jesus. Amen.

For Fathers

Good St. Joseph, the "Silent Saint," please pray to Father God, asking him to watch over the fathers of our parish. Humbled and inspired by your own example of humility, may they be chaste and prudent in all that they do. Ask the Lord to bless all fathers so that they can better live according to your will. In Jesus' name, we pray. Amen.

For Elementary, Middle, and High School Students

O Lord Jesus Christ, we know that children are so close to your heart; you said during your ministry that the kingdom of heaven belongs to them. Please watch over all of our elementary, middle, and high school students, drawing them to be your current disciples and future saints. We ask this in your holy and righteous name. Amen.

For College Students and Those Discerning What College to Attend

Heavenly Father, guide the hearts and minds of those who are in college or discerning what college to attend. Please help them to find the programs, majors, and other features that they seek. Guide their hearts to find a chapel and ministries for Catholic students wherever they land so that the Eucharist can remain at the heart of their time studying there. In the name of Jesus the Teacher, we pray. Amen.

10.

Traditional Catholic Prayers

MARIAN PRAYERS

THE ANGELUS

Leader: The Angel of the Lord declared unto Mary.

Respondents: And she conceived of the Holy Spirit.

Everyone: Hail, Mary, full of grace, the Lord is with thee. Blessed art thou among women, and blessed is the fruit of thy womb, Jesus. Holy Mary, Mother of God, pray for us sinners, now and at the hour of our death. Amen.

Leader: Behold, the handmaid of the Lord.

Respondents: Be it done unto me according to thy word.

Everyone: Hail, Mary, full of grace, the Lord is with thee . . .

Leader: And the Word was made flesh.

Respondents: And dwelt among us.

Everyone: Hail, Mary, full of grace, the Lord is with thee . . .

Leader: Pray for us, O holy Mother of God.

Respondents: That we may be made worthy of the promises of Christ.

Everyone: Pour forth, we beseech thee, O Lord, thy grace into our hearts; that we, to whom the Incarnation of Christ, thy Son, was made known by the message of an angel, may by his Passion and Cross be brought to the glory of his Resurrection. Through the same Christ our Lord. Amen.

THE HAIL, HOLY QUEEN (SALVE REGINA)

Hail, Holy Queen, Mother of Mercy, our life, our sweetness, and our hope. To thee do we cry, poor banished children of Eve. To thee do we send up our sighs, mourning and weeping in this valley of tears. Turn then, most gracious advocate, thine eyes of mercy toward us, and after this our exile, show unto us the blessed fruit of thy womb, Jesus. O clement, O loving, O sweet Virgin Mary. Pray for us, O holy Mother of God, that we may be made worthy of the promises of Christ. Amen.

THE LITANY OF LORETO

Leader: Lord, have mercy.

Respondents: Christ, have mercy.

Leader: Lord, have mercy. Christ, hear us.

Respondents: Christ, graciously hear us.

Leader: God the Father of heaven . . .

Respondents: Have mercy on us.

Leader: God the Son, Redeemer of the world . . .
Respondents: Have mercy on us.
Leader: God the Holy Spirit . . .
Respondents: Have mercy on us.
Leader: Holy Trinity, one God . . .
Respondents: Have mercy on us.
[For the remainder of the prayer, the leader provides the Marian title and the respondents answer with "pray for us."]
Holy Mary, *pray for us.*
Holy Mother of God, *pray for us.*
Holy Virgin of Virgins, *pray for us.*
Mother of Christ, *pray for us.*
Mother of divine grace, *pray for us.*
Mother most pure, *pray for us.*
Mother most chaste, *pray for us.*
Mother inviolate, *pray for us.*
Mother undefiled, *pray for us.*
Mother most amiable, *pray for us.*
Mother most admirable, *pray for us.*
Mother of good counsel, *pray for us.*
Mother of our Creator, *pray for us.*
Mother of our Savior, *pray for us.*
Virgin most prudent, *pray for us.*
Virgin most venerable, *pray for us.*
Virgin most renowned, *pray for us.*
Virgin most powerful, *pray for us.*
Virgin most merciful, *pray for us.*
Virgin most faithful, *pray for us.*
Mirror of justice, *pray for us.*

Seat of wisdom, *pray for us.*

Cause of our joy, *pray for us.*

Spiritual vessel, *pray for us.*

Vessel of honor, *pray for us.*

Singular vessel of devotion, *pray for us.*

Mystical rose, *pray for us.*

Tower of David, *pray for us.*

Tower of ivory, *pray for us.*

House of gold, *pray for us.*

Ark of the covenant, *pray for us.*

Gate of heaven, *pray for us.*

Morning star, *pray for us.*

Health of the sick, *pray for us.*

Refuge of sinners, *pray for us.*

Comforter of the afflicted, *pray for us.*

Help of Christians, *pray for us.*

Queen of Angels, *pray for us.*

Queen of Patriarchs, *pray for us.*

Queen of Prophets, *pray for us.*

Queen of Apostles, *pray for us.*

Queen of Martyrs, *pray for us.*

Queen of Confessors, *pray for us.*

Queen of Virgins, *pray for us.*

Queen of All Saints, *pray for us.*

Queen conceived without original sin, *pray for us.*

Queen assumed into heaven, *pray for us.*

Queen of the most holy Rosary, *pray for us.*

Queen of families, *pray for us.*

Queen of peace, *pray for us.*

Leader: Lamb of God, who takes away the sins of the world . . .

Respondents: Spare us, O Lord.

Leader: Lamb of God, who takes away the sins of the world . . .

Respondents: Graciously hear us, O Lord.

Leader: Lamb of God, who takes away the sins of the world . . .

Respondents: Have mercy on us.

Leader: Let us pray. Grant, we beseech thee, O Lord God, that we, thy servants, may enjoy perpetual health of mind and body, and by the glorious intercession of Blessed Mary, ever Virgin, may we be freed from present sorrow and rejoice in eternal happiness. Through Christ our Lord.

Everyone: Amen.

THE MAGNIFICAT

My soul proclaims the greatness of the Lord;
my spirit rejoices in God my Savior.
For he has looked upon his handmaid's lowliness;
behold, from now on will all ages call me blessed.
The Mighty One has done great things for me,
and holy is his name.
His mercy is from age to age
to those who fear him.
He has shown might with his arm,
dispersed the arrogant of mind and heart.
He has thrown down the rulers from their thrones,
but lifted up the lowly.
The hungry he has filled with good things;
the rich he has sent away empty.
He has helped Israel his servant,

remembering his mercy,
according to his promise to our fathers,
to Abraham and to his descendants forever. (Luke 1:46–55)

THE MEMORARE

Remember, O most gracious Virgin Mary, that never was it known that anyone who fled to your protection, implored your help, or sought your intercession was left unaided. Inspired by this confidence, I fly unto you, O Virgin of virgins, my mother. To you do I come, before you I stand, sinful and sorrowful. O Mother of the Word Incarnate, despise not my petitions, but in your mercy, hear and answer me. Amen.

THE REGINA CAELI (QUEEN OF HEAVEN)

Leader: Queen of heaven, rejoice, alleluia.

Respondents: The Son you merited to bear, alleluia.

Leader: Has risen as he said, alleluia.

Respondents: Pray to God for us, alleluia.

Leader: Rejoice and be glad, O Virgin Mary, alleluia.

Respondents: For the Lord has truly risen, alleluia.

Leader: Let us pray. God of life, you have given joy to the world by the Resurrection of your Son, our Lord Jesus Christ. Through the prayers of his mother, the Virgin Mary, bring us to the happiness of eternal life. We ask this through Christ our Lord. Amen.

ANYTIME PRAYERS

ANIMA CHRISTI

Soul of Christ, sanctify me. Body of Christ, save me. Blood of Christ, inebriate me. Water from the side of Christ, wash me. Passion of Christ, strengthen me. O good Jesus, hear me. Within Thy wounds, hide me. Separated from Thee, let me never be. From the malignant enemy, defend me. At the hour of death, call me. And close to Thee, bid me. That with Thy saints, I may be praising Thee, forever and ever. Amen.

THE DIVINE PRAISES

Blessed be God.
Blessed be his holy Name.
Blessed be Jesus Christ, true God and true Man.
Blessed be the name of Jesus.
Blessed be his most Sacred Heart.
Blessed be his most Precious Blood.
Blessed be Jesus in the most holy Sacrament of the altar.
Blessed be the Holy Spirit, the Paraclete.
Blessed be the great Mother of God, Mary most holy.
Blessed be her holy and Immaculate Conception.
Blessed be her glorious Assumption.
Blessed be the name of Mary, Virgin and Mother.
Blessed be St. Joseph, her most chaste spouse.
Blessed be God in his angels and in his saints.

THE DOXOLOGY (THE GLORY BE)

Glory be to the Father, and to the Son, and to the Holy Spirit, as it was in the beginning, is now, and ever shall be, world without end. Amen.

THE FÁTIMA PRAYER

O my Jesus, forgive us our sins, and save us from the fires of hell. Lead all souls to heaven, especially those in most need of thy mercy. Amen.

GUARDIAN ANGEL PRAYER

Angel of God, my guardian dear, to whom God's love commits me here, ever this day be at my side, to light and guard, to rule and guide. Amen.

THE LORD'S PRAYER (THE OUR FATHER)

Our Father, who art in heaven, hallowed be thy name. Thy kingdom come. Thy will be done, on earth as it is in heaven. Give us this day our daily bread, and forgive us our trespasses, as we forgive those who trespass against us, and lead us not into temptation, but deliver us from evil. Amen.

PRAYER FOR THE FAITHFUL DEPARTED

Eternal rest grant unto them, O Lord, and let perpetual light shine upon them. May they rest in peace. Amen.

PRAYER TO THE HOLY SPIRIT

Leader: Come, Holy Spirit, fill the hearts of your faithful.

Respondents: And kindle in them the fire of your love.

Leader: Send forth your Spirit, and they shall be created.

Respondents: And you shall renew the face of the earth.

PRAYER FOR PEACE (PEACE PRAYER OF ST. FRANCIS)

Lord, make me an instrument of your peace.
Where there is hatred, let me sow love;
where there is injury, pardon;
where there is doubt, faith; where there is despair, hope;
where there is darkness, light; and where there is sadness, joy.
O Divine Master, grant that I may not so much seek
to be consoled as to console,
to be understood as to understand, to be loved as to love;
for it is in giving that we receive,
it is in pardoning that we are pardoned,
and it is in dying that we are born to eternal life.
Amen.

PRAYER TO ST. MICHAEL THE ARCHANGEL

St. Michael the Archangel, defend us in battle. Be our protection against the wickedness and snares of the devil. May God rebuke him, we humbly pray. And do thou, O Prince of the Heavenly Host, by the power of God, thrust into hell Satan and all evil spirits who wander the earth seeking the ruin of souls. Amen.

St. Augustine of Hippo's Prayer to the Holy Spirit

Breathe in me, O Holy Spirit, that my thoughts may all be holy.
Act in me, O Holy Spirit, that my work, too, may be holy.
Draw my heart, O Holy Spirit, that I love but what is holy.
Strengthen me, O Holy Spirit, to defend all that is holy.
Guard me, then, O Holy Spirit, that I always may be holy.
Amen.

An Act of Contrition

O my God, I am heartily sorry for having offended you, and I detest all my sins because I dread the loss of heaven and the pains of hell, but most of all because they offend you, my God, who are all good and deserving of all my love. I firmly resolve, with the help of your grace, to confess my sins, do penance, and amend my life. Amen.

An Act of Faith, Hope, and Love

Jesus, I believe in you. Jesus, I hope in you. Jesus, I love you. Amen.

An Act of Faith

Oh my God, I firmly believe that you are one God in three divine Persons, Father, Son, and Holy Spirit. I believe that your divine Son became man and died for our sins, and that he will come to judge the living and the dead. I believe these and all the truths which the Holy Catholic Church teaches, because you have revealed them, who are eternal truth and wisdom, who can neither deceive nor be deceived. In this faith I intend to live and die. Amen.

An Act of Hope

O Lord God, I hope by your grace for the pardon of all my sins, and after life here to gain eternal happiness, because you have promised it, who are infinitely powerful, faithful, kind, and merciful. In this hope I intend to live and die. Amen.

An Act of Love

O Lord God, I love you above all things, and I love my neighbor for your sake, because you are the highest, infinite, and perfect good, worthy of all my love. In this love I intend to live and die. Amen.

PRAYERS FOR SET TIMES

Morning Offering

O Jesus, through the Immaculate Heart of Mary, I offer you my prayers, works, joys, and sufferings of this day, for all the intentions of your Sacred Heart, in union with the Holy Sacrifice of the Mass throughout the world, for the salvation of souls, the reparation of sins, the reunion of all Christians, and in particular for the intentions of the Holy Father this month. Amen.

Morning Prayer

God our Father, I offer you today all that I think and do and say. I offer it with what was done on earth by Jesus Christ, your Son. Amen.

Evening Prayer

God our Father, this day is done. We ask you and Jesus Christ, your Son, that with the Spirit, our welcome guest, you guard our sleep and bless our rest. Amen.

Grace before Meals

Bless us, O Lord, and these, thy gifts, which we are about to receive from thy bounty, through Christ our Lord. Amen.

Grace after Meals

We give thanks, almighty God, for these and all the gifts which we have received from your goodness, through Christ our Lord. Amen.

The Hail Mary

Hail, Mary, full of grace, the Lord is with thee. Blessed art thou among women, and blessed is the fruit of thy womb, Jesus. Holy Mary, Mother of God, pray for us sinners, now and at the hour of our death. Amen.

CREEDS

THE APOSTLES' CREED

I believe in God,
the Father almighty,
Creator of heaven and earth,
and in Jesus Christ, his only Son, our Lord,
[At the following words, up to and including "the Virgin Mary,"
all bow.]
who was conceived by the Holy Spirit,
born of the Virgin Mary,
suffered under Pontius Pilate,
was crucified, died, and was buried;
he descended into hell;
on the third day, he rose again from the dead;
he ascended into heaven,
and is seated at the right hand of God, the Father almighty;
from there he will come to judge the living and the dead.

I believe in the Holy Spirit,
the holy Catholic Church,
the Communion of Saints,
the forgiveness of sins,
the resurrection of the body,
and life everlasting. Amen.

The Nicene Creed

I believe in one God,
the Father almighty,
maker of heaven and earth,
of all things visible and invisible.

I believe in one Lord Jesus Christ,
the Only Begotten Son of God,
born of the Father before all ages.
God from God, Light from Light,
true God from true God,
begotten, not made, consubstantial with the Father;
through him, all things were made.
For us men, and for our salvation
he came down from heaven,
[At the following words, up to and including "and became man,"
all bow.]
and by the Holy Spirit was incarnate of the Virgin Mary,
and became man.
For our sake, he was crucified under Pontius Pilate,
he suffered death and was buried,
and rose again on the third day
in accordance with the scriptures.
He ascended into heaven
and is seated at the right hand of the Father.
He will come again in glory
to judge the living and the dead
and his kingdom will have no end.

I believe in the Holy Spirit, the Lord, the giver of life,
who proceeds from the Father and the Son,
who with the Father and the Son is adored and glorified,
who has spoken through the prophets.

I believe in one, holy, catholic, and apostolic Church.
I confess one Baptism for the forgiveness of sins
and I look forward to the resurrection of the dead
and the life of the world to come. Amen.

Appendix

Writing Prayers for Your Group's Gathering

We are always encouraged to write our own prayers. The prayers in this book cover myriad situations within a Catholic parish, but they are ultimately examples that you could expand, condense, or otherwise adapt for the particular needs of your community. The four types of prayer in the Catholic tradition are *adoration* (attentively giving praise to God), *contrition* (pleading to God for him to forgive us), *petition* (making a reasonable, noble request of God), and *thanksgiving* (expressing our true gratitude to God). A few principles to remember when writing your own prayers are fidelity, focus, simplicity, and sincerity.

Fidelity

Ensure that your prayer is faithful to the Church's teachings.
Few things are more jarring than being in a prayer setting and
hearing an errant—or even heretical—prayer that cannot be
aligned with the various doctrines and practices of the Church.
You may miss your great Aunt Sally dearly, but praying to God
for her to come back from the dead and provide her input in
person at a parish council meeting would of course be inappro-
priate (and, yes, laughable). When in doubt, show your prayer
to a priest or other trusted member of your parish staff before
offering it in a public setting or allowing it to be printed.

Focus

Make sure that your prayer is addressed to God. You might be
surprised at how often a prayer leader begins by addressing the
gathered and simply continues focused on them. As Catholics
our communal prayer begins by addressing God and then typ-
ically offers a word of praise or thanksgiving or simply states
the condition of the people gathered. In short, focus on God
and remain on topic.

For example, when offering a prayer of thanksgiving for
the completion of a new Catholic school building containing
seventy-five different academic rooms, it is unnecessary to ask
God to bless every single room by listing them by name. Focus,
rather, on asking the Lord's blessings upon the Catholic educational institution as a whole. Be sure to read the prayer to

yourself a few times to make sure that it is relevant—not too vague or sterile but also not so specific as to read as a self-centered pleading. When we pray, we cast our vision wide.

Simplicity

Prayer, particularly within a public setting such as a parish event, is an opportunity to draw everyone's thoughts heavenward. However, it is not a time to "show off" or otherwise draw attention to yourself. Make sure that your prayer is simple without being too *simplistic* or overly revelatory of your personal concerns or details of your life. Your prayer should provoke your fellow parishioners' hearts and minds to consider heavenly truths without making them feel intellectually inferior on the one hand or not challenged at all on the other.

Sincerity

Ultimately, a prayer should be sincere in its scope and its intent (think of the significance of the term *intention*). According to the *Catechism of the Catholic Church*, St. John Damascene famously described prayer as "the raising of one's mind and heart to God or the requesting of good things from God" (*CCC* 2559). Keeping that definition in mind, consider what your goal is in communicating with God and opening yourself up to his will in your life, and make sure you know what you want your prayer to convey.

Use the occasion of writing a prayer to draw yourself and your parish community to reflect on God's goodness and his will for you. Be creative. Be confident. Be clear. Be charitable. And of course, pray to God—especially in front of the Blessed Sacrament during eucharistic adoration—for an outpouring of the Holy Spirit to help you write your prayer(s). Then begin!

Index

Gregory Nazianzen and Basil the Great, Sts., Memorial of (Jan. 2), 38

Gregory the Great, St., Memorial of (Sept. 3), 62

growing season, 18, 21

Guardian Angel Prayer, 180

guest speakers, 106

Hail, Holy Queen (Salve Regina), 174

Hail Mary, 184

Halloween (Oct. 31), 35

harvest, 21

Holy Body and Blood of Christ, Solemnity of, 34

Holy Family, Feast of, 28

Holy Guardian Angels, Memorial of the (Oct. 2), 67

Holy Innocents, Feast of (Dec. 28), 27

Holy Spirit, gifts of, 148–150

Holy Trinity, Solemnity of, 33

Holy Week, 30–31

homeless people, 14–15, 144

hope, 118, 123, 138

hospitality ministers, 93–94

household unity, 118–119

humility, 122

Ignatius of Antioch, St., Memorial of (Oct. 17), 69

Ignatius of Loyola, St., Memorial of (July 31), 56

illness, 14, 125

Immaculate Conception of the Virgin Mary, Solemnity of (Dec. 8), 23, 78

Incarnation, gratitude for, 25–26

Independence Day (July 4), 82–83

infertility, 125–126

international crises, 132–133

internet use, 133

Irenaeus, St., Memorial of (June 28), 52

Isaac Jogues, Jean de Brébeuf, and Companions, Sts., Memorial of (Oct. 19), 69

Isidore, St., Memorial of (May 15), 49

isolation, 124

James, St., Feast of (July 25), 55

James and Philip, Sts., Memorial of (May 3), 48

January

    Day of Prayer for the Legal Protection of Unborn Children (Jan. 22), 40

    Epiphany, 28

    Feast of the Baptism of the Lord, 28

    Feast of the Conversion of St. Paul the Apostle (Jan. 25), 41

    Martin Luther King Jr. Day, 81–82

    Memorial of Bl. Basil Moreau (Jan. 20), 39

    Memorial of St. Agnes (Jan. 21), 40

    Memorial of St. André Bessette (Jan. 6), 39

    Memorial of St. Anthony (Jan. 17), 39

    Memorial of St. Elizabeth Ann Seton (Jan. 4), 38

    Memorial of St. Francis de Sales (Jan. 24), 41

    Memorial of St. John Neumann (Jan. 5), 38

    Memorial of St. Marianne Cope (Jan. 23), 40

    Memorial of St. Thomas Aquinas (Jan. 28), 42

    Memorial of Sts. Basil the Great and Gregory Nazianzen (Jan. 2), 38